WONDERFUL WORLD OF KNOWLEDGE

The Far West

Disney's

Wonderful
World of
Knowledge

THE DANBURY PRESS

THE DANBURY PRESS

a division of Grolier Enterprises, Inc.

ROBERT B. CLARKE   *Publisher*

ARNOLDO MONDADORI EDITORE

MARIO GENTILINI	*Editor-in-Chief*
ELISA PENNA	*Supervising Editor*
GIOVAN BATTISTA CARPI	*Illustrators*
GUIDO MARTINA	*Author*

ISBN 0-7172-8102-7
"Disney's WONDERFUL WORLD OF KNOWLEDGE"
is an updated and enlarged English version of
an encyclopedia heretofore printed in the Italian language by
ARNOLDO MONDADORI EDITORE, MILAN
and entitled (in English Translation) "Disney ENCYCLOPEDIA"

CONTENTS

THE FAR WEST

West of the Mississippi, the Rocky Mountains rise from the Great Plains. Still farther west lies the shoreline of the Pacific Ocean. Here is the territory that has gone down in history and legend as the land of adventure: the fabulous West, the frontier where. . . .

"Hey, Donald, start over! First you have to say what you're talking about. That 'fabulous West' doesn't exist now. It hasn't existed since 1890. That was the year the United States Bureau of the Census declared that there was no more frontier. Before then, any place with fewer than two white people per square mile was called the West. Those two palefaces were usually explorers, pioneers, guides, fur traders, gold hunters, missionaries. . . ."

That was Daisy, boys and girls. She likes to interrupt and also to ask questions. It's a good idea. If people ask questions as we go along, we can be sure everyone understands what I'm telling you about the West.

And of course I'm your friend Donald. You've probably guessed that already, because you know you usually find me with Daisy at my side. I have a lot of fun telling you these stories. Daisy has fun asking questions and we both hope you will have fun being with us on our western adventure.

But I think I'll take Daisy's advice and start over at the beginning.

THE TREASURE-HUNTERS

From the start, the New World was a great temptation to Spanish conquistadores (conquerors). Greedy for gold, they conquered the Aztecs of Mexico and the Incas of Peru, killing people and seizing their treasures. Then they looked around for more treasures. It was rumored that north of Mexico, in our old West, lay the Seven Cities of Cíbola. It was said that they had walls of gold and emerald-studded gates. A Franciscan missionary, Marcos de Niza, had lived with the Indians and heard them talk about the cities. One day he even thought he saw their golden walls gleaming in the distance!

Unlike the friendlier Hopi, the Apache and Comanche Indians of the Great Plains fought bravely against the Spanish conquistadores and forced them to retreat.

You can guess how excited the Spaniards were when they heard this. So early in 1540 Francisco Vásquez de Coronado set out to find Cíbola. He led an expedition of about 300 Spanish horsemen and hundreds of Indians, with Friar Marcos as guide. In July of that year, after many hardships, they reached the hill where the Friar had stood when he thought he saw the gleaming walls. Imagine their rage when they found only a poor Zuni Indian village! No trace of gold or jewels!

Was Marcos fooled by the sun flashing on mud huts? Perhaps. In any event he was sent back to Mexico in disgrace. But the Spaniards cheered up when they captured an Indian who told them of the magical land of Quivira. They called their captive the Turk because he looked like one. In all probability he was a Pawnee Indian. Far out on the Great Plains, the Turk said, was Quivira, where everyone ate from plates of gold. There flowed a river 7 miles wide, where fish as big as horses swam. The king rested each day under a tree whose branches were hung with tiny golden bells. The bells chimed in the breeze to give him sweet dreams.

The expedition set off eagerly for Quivira, with the Turk as guide. For months the treasure-seekers wandered.

Finally Coronado reached Quivira—but

The Spanish conquistador Francisco Vásquez de Coronado (above) was one of the first Europeans to venture from the South into the West. He was searching for the legendary Seven Cities of Cibola, with their walls of gold. Another Spaniard, Hernando de Soto, made the same futile search. Both of these explorers went as far as present-day Oklahoma and were among the first white men to enter the heartland of the United States.

A view of the wild natural beauty of the Grand Canyon.

alas, there was no gold. He found only a few mud huts belonging to the Wichita Indians, in what is now Kansas. Under torture the Turk confessed that the Pueblo Indians had used him to lead the Spaniards on a wild-goose chase. The Indians hoped that the Spaniards would get lost and starve.

The Spaniards took revenge on the Turk by strangling him. Then they headed back for Mexico, because they had very little food and supplies. Since they had wanted only treasure, they felt like failures. They did not realize that the grass of the Plains offered fine pasture, or that the buffalo were a rich source of food. They took no pride in having explored much of the Southwest, or in the fact that some of them had been the first white men ever to see the Grand Canyon!

DANGER ON THE PLAINS

The Southwest Indians belonged to many tribes—Zuni and Hopi, among others. The Spaniards called these Indians Pueblo ("village") because of the way they lived. They lived in many-storied clay "apartment houses." The roof of one home formed the porch for the family living above. There were few doors or windows in the houses. The people entered by climbing ladders and going through holes in the roofs. During an attack, they could pull up the ladders and be safe. The Pueblo Indians didn't like fighting and killing. They were farmers who grew corn, squash, beans, and cotton. They liked to weave bright cloth and make turquoise jewelry and beautiful pottery.

The Mississippi River, Great Father of Waters, has its source in Lake Itasca in Minnesota. The Spaniards, the first white men to see the river, kept its discovery a secret, and almost a whole century passed before it was rediscovered by the French. Ocean liners can sail up the Mississippi for a distance of about 100 miles from its mouth.

So you see they were a skilled people. Also, they had learned from sad experience that the white men sometimes tortured and killed their people. Since they didn't like fighting, they deceived the white men with stories of gold that was to be found somewhere far from their village.

Fooled by such reports, the Spaniards would hurry off to the Great Plains. There, as the Pueblo had hoped, the white men met some very different Indians. These were Apache and Comanche. They were fierce warriors who hid behind rocks and sent arrows winging into the invading Spaniards.

The Spaniards took to their heels and ran home to Mexico. There they spread the word about the "Apache terror." After that, expeditions made a big circle to avoid the Great Plains.

But now let us venture boldly onto the

13

Plains and meet those fierce defenders, the Apache and Comanche.

WELCOME, HORSE

Can you imagine an Indian without his horse? Yet no Indian had ever seen a horse before the white man came. To pull loads, the Indians used a hauling device called a travois. They hunted buffalo and fought enemies on foot. You can see that they were at a great disadvantage in their first battles with the Spaniards, who were on horseback. The Indians quickly learned the value of horses for hunting and war.

After the Spaniards settled New Mexico early in the 17th century, Apache raiding parties began stealing horses. Horses that escaped from their owners formed wild herds (mustangs), which the Indians caught and trained. Soon the Apache became fine horsemen, the terror of both white and Indian enemies.

The Indians grew rich, for with horses they could catch many more buffalo. Colts specially branded or marked with ear slits were trained to sniff out buffalo, chase them, and make lightning dashes to escape a maddened buffalo's charge.

The Apache prized his war-horse above all else. He wove feathers into its mane and hung bear-claw necklaces around its neck. The horse was trained to let a wounded warrior cling to its tail and be dragged to safety. Sometimes a warrior brought a spare horse to battle, in case his war-horse was shot and the rider needed to make a fast getaway. Though they were

The remains of the Alamo mission in San Antonio, Texas. In 1836 the 187 Texans defending the mission died after fighting 12 days against 5,000 Mexicans. Davy Crockett, the famous hunter and politician, was one of the victims.

brave warriors, Indians never forgot that the warrior who survives can fight another day.

"They brought spare horses to buffalo hunts too, Donald. The hunter rode an old pack horse to the hunt and saved his fast horse for the chase. Are you going to tell us how the warrior rode in battle?"

Yes, Daisy, I am. Those Indians were daredevil riders. The Indian jumped onto his horse's back while it was running. Then he slipped down to cling flat against the horse's side as it galloped. The horse's body was his shield against enemy arrows. To hold on, he dug his heel into the horse's back. He could swivel on that heel, reach the top of the horse, then drop and hang down on the opposite side. This left his hands free for his bow and arrow. Hidden from attackers by his horse, he could shoot arrows under the horse's neck as he galloped past his enemy! How's that for a dandy trick?

"I'd like to see you do it!"

That Daisy! She knows very well that I could do it if I were an Apache or Comanche warrior on the Great Plains.

IF I WERE AN INDIAN WARRIOR

If I were an Indian warrior I'd have to make all my own weapons. That was the unbreakable rule on the Great Plains.

"Why did they have that rule?"

Because the Indian thought that if he received his weapons as gifts, or if he bought them, they would be powerless in battle. He gave them power by making them himself.

And let me add that if we were Indians, Daisy would have to help me by making my clothes. Indians squaws worked very hard dressing buffalo skins and sewing war gear by hand with bone needles. They used buffalo sinews for thread. They made leather chaps and moccasins, and beaded headbands. The warriors attached their warbonnets to these bands. The bonnet was made of eagle feathers, sometimes trimmed with white weasel tails or red flannel, and it might go clear down his back. But it was more than an ornament. It was a badge of honor, and it told people many things about its brave wearer.

Another badge of honor was the staff, a spear trimmed with a feather. Touching

a live enemy with it and getting away was considered a coup (glorious deed). He might touch a foe lying on the ground just pretending to be dead, waiting for a chance to rise up and kill. After the battle, the braves got together to see who had the most coups. Killing an enemy single-handed was a coup. So was stealing his weapons.

The Plains Indians used bows made of driftwood, horn, or bone. The bows were joined with leather thongs and were shaped like the Cupid's bow we see on Valentine's Day. Bows were short, no more than three feet. For a man on horse-back, a short bow was easier to handle than a long one. Arrows were feathered at one end to guide them to their mark. Arrow-heads were chipped from flint, horn, or bone. Later they were made of iron, taken from the hoops of white men's barrels.

Some tribes had two kinds of arrows. One was the buffalo arrow for hunting. Its arrowheads were firmly bound to the shaft with thongs and glue. The Indian could hit a buffalo at a distance of over 65 feet. He aimed for a spot between the shoulders and neck of the animal, hoping his arrow would go through the heart. Each Indian put his mark on his arrows, so he could tell which buffalo he'd killed. He would then save the arrows to use again.

The man arrow was for war. Some-times its arrowhead was tied loosely to the shaft so that it would come off when the victim tried to pull the arrow out. Then the arrowhead stayed in the wound, thus adding to the injury.

Indians held special ceremonies to give

Left: Monument Valley, where the Navajo settled, lies on the border between Utah and Arizona.

17

Plains Indians in war paint and full regalia lead the opening parade of the annual Pendleton Roundup in Oregon. Every year Indians from many of the reservations take part in festivals such as this one. Most of the traditions of the past are no longer observed. But these yearly festivals serve as colorful reminders of the Indian customs of hundreds of years ago.

their warriors and weapons magic powers. Before the summer hunt, Plains Indians held a sun dance that lasted several days. Its aim was to ask the Great Spirit to give them many buffalo. Some tribes held a buffalo dance, wearing buffalo masks. Each warrior had a "medicine bundle." In it were objects that a spirit had shown

18

him in a dream. He believed it gave him power in battle. No Blackfoot warrior would go into battle without his "war medicine." He usually got it from an older war hero, who prayed over the object and with it transferred some of his own power to the young brave. It might be a feather, a knife, or a necklace.

The warrior carried his arrows in a quiver made of buffalo hide, slung over his shoulder. It hung near the hand that pulled the bowstring, so he could reach his arrows in a hurry. Even with his horse at full gallop, he could shoot fast enough to keep an arrow always flying!

On his other arm, the brave wore a small round shield. It was painted with magic designs for extra protection. As he advanced, he held the shield close to him. Escaping, he let it swing loosely at his back to ward off arrows, spears, or bullets fired at him from behind.

This was the fierce horseman of the West. The white man had much to learn before he could conquer such a skilled warrior. But remember that the Indian was fighting to defend himself, his home, and his buffalo herds. Most important, the white man had to learn the secrets of the Indian's battlefield, the Great Plains.

THE KEY TO THE PUZZLE

If we were to take a look at the map of North America, we would see a big area west of the Mississippi, stretching from Canada to Mexico. That was the home of more than 31 Indian tribes with different languages. Among the more advanced of the Great Plains Indians were the following 11 tribes: Assiniboin, Arapaho, Blackfoot, Cheyenne, Comanche, Crow, Hidatsa (also called Gros Ventre), Apache, Sarsi, Shoshone, and Dakota, or Sioux. Later I'll explain what some of the names mean.

"Why later? Why not now?"

Because, Daisy, I'm saving a whole chapter later on for Indian names. I ask you, did you ever see such an impatient woman? You see, first I want to solve the mystery of the Great Plains.

"Oh, good, I love mysteries. What's this one about?"

Here we go. Since most of these tribes spoke their own languages—each different from any other—how did they talk to each other? Don't ponder, there's a simple explanation. The Indians talked sign language when they met others from different tribes. Everybody on the Great Plains knew what the hand-signals meant.

Yes, that's how they understood each other when they met face to face. But suppose they wanted to send news to a far-off place? They had no writing, no post office, and of course no telephone. It took white men a long time to figure out how the Indians sent news. But the answer was right in front of their eyes. All they would have had to do was look at the ground or the sky near the hills. You tell me, Daisy.

"The Indians lit bonfires with green twigs and wet straw. That made a smoky fire on a hilltop. Then they waved a rug over the fire. They made big smoke puffs and little ones that spelled out a message in code. At night they built bright fires with dry wood, and waved the blanket over the flames and smoke. That made a blinking kind of code."

Very good, Daisy. But we are talking about the Great Plains, where there was very little wood to make a fire. How did they send a message if they had no wood? Everybody give up? OK, I'll tell you.

The horsemen of the Plains worked out

Every year during the month of August, people from all over the Southwest gather in Gallup, New Mexico, to take part in a re-enactment of pioneer life. The festival is a popular tourist attraction.

A scene at the festival in Gallup, New Mexico. Before the Indians had any knowledge of the wheel, they used these stretcherlike sleds, called travois, for transportation. Originally these sleds were drawn by dogs, and later by horses. The poles were often used to support tents.

a very clever code of their own. Colonel Richard I. Dodge told about it in his book, *Hunting Grounds of the Great West*.

The Colonel was out riding one day with a band of Sioux warriors. There were about a hundred braves on horseback. For half an hour he watched the braves going through a strange kind of drill. Their chief stood on a slight rise 700 feet away and led the braves through their paces. The horses marched and turned in a pattern so complex that the Colonel marveled. He thought no cavalry in the world could equal this. He watched the chief carefully, but all he could see was a slight movement of the chief's right hand.

"Please teach me your system," he said to the chief.

The chief said he could not do that. It was "sacred magic," and if he told an outsider, it would bring the tribe bad luck. All the Colonel could find out was that the chief was holding a little mirror in his hand.

Now do you know how the Indians sent their messages?

A FOUR-LEGGED WIRELESS

So now that I've explained the mysterious secret. . . .

"You call *that* explaining? All I heard

was something about some horses marching around. What does that have to do with sending messages? I suppose you'll give us the same answer as the chief: magic. Well, I don't believe it."

Daisy, sometimes you don't see the answer when it's right under your nose. Try to guess.

"Maybe the chief was flashing code with that little mirror?"

That's a good guess. But the chief was just using the mirror to guide his horsemen. When the Indians had no wood for fires and no mirrors and no sun to make flashes, then how did they send messages?

Give up? Everybody give up? All right, they used their horses.

"The horses sent messages? Come on!"

Yes, indeed, the horses sent the messages. And this is how they did it. The

A scene at the Pendleton Roundup. Indian shelters, called tipis or tepees by the Sioux and wigwams by the Algonkin, were usually made of buffalo hide supported by 3 to 16 poles. Those pictured here are modern adaptations.

24

Indians rode their horses up to the top of the hill. There they marched their horses in a pattern. It might be just one horse going through special movements. Each movement had its own meaning for the faraway watcher. If an Indian had no horse, he could send messages by his own movements. Running back and forth meant he'd seen the enemy. Holding a blanket up and bringing it down meant: buffalo herd.

Is it any wonder the U.S. Army often used Indian guides? An Army officer reported that he could hardly see the hilltop and its horsemen, even with field glasses. Yet beside him the Indian guide was busily reporting the news that the distant rider was sending!

Above: Pueblo Indians of Taos, New Mexico. The Pueblo, a farming people, had a highly developed culture. Their social structure was a matriarchy (mothers were the heads of the families). Right: In their architecture, these Pueblo homes are very similar to those built hundreds of years ago.

FRIEND OR ENEMY?

The Great Plains, the Indians' hunting ground, became a battlefield as white men moved in to colonize it. Red men had no intention of letting it be colonized. They bitterly defended their grazing lands and their buffalo. Each side thought it was right.

Yet the two races were not always at war. There were examples of friendship, too. For instance. . . .

"Pocahontas, the Indian Princess!"

I see Daisy is in a hurry to get a woman into the story. We'll get to her soon. But let's start with a colonel.

Colonel A. G. Boove was a good friend to the Indians. He never hesitated to use his soldiers to defend the Indians against white raiders. Of course this got him into a lot of trouble with some white men who wanted the Indian lands. These men found a judge to help them. The judge worked out a plot to get rid of Boove and replace him with a soldier who would not interfere with raids. The charges brought against Boove were false, but no one cared except the Sioux.

Before this, the Sioux had buried the hatchet. That means that they had agreed not to go on the warpath against the palefaces. But they said they would *un*-bury the hatchet very fast unless their friend got a fair trial. It is said that 150 Sioux chieftains sold their horses to raise money for Boove's defense. Since you know how Indians felt about their horses, you can see how much they cared!

And that is how the Sioux took care of their friends. Among those chieftains was the famous medicine man Sitting Bull. I'm going to tell you about him next.

"Oh, no, please tell us about Pocahontas! If we don't get some girls in this story pretty soon, the girl readers are going to get angry!"

Maybe she's right. So let's come to the story of Pocahontas, part fact, part legend.

A group of Plains Indians at the Gallup festival. In the foreground are a young mother and her son. They are wearing the colorful traditional ornaments of their tribe.

29

A Navajo woman weaves one of the brightly colored blankets for which her tribe is famous.

PRINCESS POCAHONTAS

Once upon a time there was an Indian princess named Pocahontas. She lived. . . . "Was she a real princess?"

Wouldn't you know that was Daisy? She loves stories about kings and queens and princes and princesses. Pocahontas was indeed a real princess. She was the daughter of Chief Powhatan, leader of the Federation of Algonkin tribes, known as the Confederacy of Powhatan. They lived where Richmond, Virginia, is today.

The English landed near there in 1606 and founded Jamestown, their first New World colony. A year or so later the Indians saw one of the settlers, John Smith, exploring a river. They caught him and took him before Powhatan. The chief admired Smith's courage. And since he didn't want any trouble with the white men, he asked that Smith be set free. But the medicine men insisted that Smith must die. There was much argument.

While they argued, Pocahontas came creeping up to the campfire. She listened wide-eyed. She stared at the golden-haired prisoner. Never before had she

Left: An Apache shield, bow, and quiver. The arrowheads are made of stone. Left, above: A Sioux headdress. Right, above: Mandan headdress. Right, below: Blackfoot medicine man headdress. The tail is made of ermine and horns.

You have probably read in adventure stories about Indians sealing pacts of friendship by smoking a calumet, or peace pipe. Pictured above are two real Indian calumets. The bows of the pipes are made of stone. The long stems are painted and decorated with porcupine quills.

seen a white man, or any man so calm in the face of death. Her father mustn't let them kill him!

But at last Powhatan gave in to the will of the medicine men. One story tells that Smith was forced to kneel with his head on a stone to prepare for his death. Pocahontas leaped forward and threw herself across Smith, covering his head with her long black hair.

"You can't kill him! I won't let you!" she cried.

Powhatan was proud of his daughter's courage. After all, as a princess she had a right to claim a prisoner. He ordered his men to unbind Smith's arms and set him free. At least this is the way John Smith told the story in his book, but some historians aren't quite sure that that is how it happened.

31

SITTING BULL'S WINCHESTER

The famous Sioux Chief Sitting Bull surrendered this Model '66 Winchester to Major David H. Brotherton at Fort Buford, on August 20, 1881. Many Indian warriors used repeating rifles in the Plains-Indian wars of the 1870's.

At left: Indian chiefs who led their braves in the battle of the Little Bighorn, where General Custer and his men died. Top left: Crazy Horse, the chief of the Oglala Sioux. He was finally taken captive and lost his life while trying to escape. Bottom left: Sitting Bull, chief and medicine man of the Sioux. The group photograph shown above was taken in 1870 in Omaha, Nebraska. Standing in the back row are Julius Meyer, the interpreter (left), and the Indian chief Red Cloud. Seated, from left to right: Sitting Bull, Swift Bear, and Spotted Tail. Sitting Bull's Winchester rifle (above) is now in Washington's Smithsonian Institution.

A PLEDGE OF PEACE

John Smith went back to Jamestown and became leader of the colony. He saved the settlers from starving by making them grow crops, mainly tobacco, and by trading with the Indians for corn. Now that he had a friend at their camp, a princess at that, it was easy to trade.

Pocahontas came often to Jamestown to visit John Smith. She loved to listen to his stories of the white man's world far away across the sea.

But in 1609 Smith had a bad accident caused by a gunpowder keg that exploded. He was forced to return to England to be treated. Pocahontas grieved for her fair-haired friend. According to legend, she even thought he was dead. Now she never came to Jamestown anymore. The Indians grew less and less friendly with the white men. Finally war broke out between them.

In the spring of 1613 the English captured Pocahontas. They held her hostage, hoping to trade her for white prisoners that the Indians had taken. Of course, they treated her with great respect for she was the daughter of a chief.

Slowly Pocahontas grew used to the white men's ways. She became a Christian and was baptized Rebecca. Her beauty won the hearts of the bachelor settlers, and many Englishmen wished to marry her. One was John Rolfe, a bright young settler who had become a leader in the planting and curing of tobacco. This gave Jamestown a cash crop, which made the colony a success. Finally the princess accepted John. Delighted, the colonists sent word to her father.

The wedding, in April, 1614, was a huge celebration for Indians and settlers together. It put an end to the war, for now these groups were related by marriage. On

Ætatis suæ 21. Aº 1616.

One of the most romantic figures in the history of the Indians of North America was Pocahontas, daughter of Powhatan, a chief of the Algonkin. According to the well-known story, Pocahontas saved the life of the British colonist John Smith. When she heard that Powhatan and his council had condemned Smith to death, the brave young girl came to his rescue and won him his freedom. Later Pocahontas went to England as the bride of a British gentleman, and was presented to the queen. This portrait was painted in England. Pocahontas died at the age of 22.

his daughter's wedding day, Powhatan said, "The battle-ax has fallen from my hands and the time of blood has ended!"

Once again Pocahontas had brought good luck to Jamestown. Her marriage to Rolfe was a pledge of peace between red man and white man.

She gave something more to Virginia, for she and Rolfe had a son, Thomas. Many famous Virginians claim to be de-

33

scended from Thomas and his royal mother. Two of them were John Randolph, a signer of the Declaration of Independence, and Edith Galt, wife of President Woodrow Wilson and one of America's first ladies.

ROYALTY MEETS ROYALTY

Proud of his princess, John Rolfe wanted his friends across the sea to know her. They sailed for England, the land John Smith had told her about long ago. There she received a royal reception. Even Queen Anne wished to meet her. She was presented at court, wearing English court dress: a long gown and stiff white lace collar. The Queen politely welcomed her as a princess of an allied nation and everyone gave parties for her.

There is a legend that she met John Smith at a party and learned for the first time that he was not dead. They say she was overcome with emotion, for she still loved the man whose life she had saved when she was a child.

This is probably not true. But it is true that the English made a great pet of her. After all, she was the first American princess they had ever seen! Maybe they even "loved her to death." Their society life was a startling change for a girl from Virginia's forests. In 1617 she sickened and died. She was only 22 years old.

John Rolfe went sadly back to Jamestown. Often Pocahontas had brought luck to the settlers. Perhaps Rolfe lost his luck when he lost his princess. He was killed by Indians in the uprising of 1622.

But Pocahontas has led us far from the land of the buffalo. It is time to go west again, back to the Great Plains.

Red Cloud, a Sioux chief, was one of the white man's bitterest enemies. In 1866 he led a group of Indians in an attack known as the Fetterman massacre, in which 80 of their American opponents lost their lives.

Above: Sketch drawn by Sioux chief Sitting Bull. The buffalo (upper right) was his symbol. He is pictured defending himself from an enemy. Below, left: Sequoya, the famous Cherokee who devised an alphabet for his people. Around his neck is the medal he received for his accomplishment. Center: Chief Joseph of the Nez Percé, who led a group of Indians to Canada in search of fair treatment. Right: The Apache leader Geronimo. After the cruel slaying of his wife and children, Geronimo sought revenge by terrorizing white settlements. Opposite page: Two Indian belts ornamented with wampum, or shell-bead, symbols. Since the Indians were not able to write, they exchanged these belts when peace treaties were signed. The one shown at left was used to conclude the peace between William Penn and the Delaware Indians in 1682. Below the belts is the document giving the English translation. The terms of this treaty were strictly honored by both Indians and Americans during Penn's lifetime.

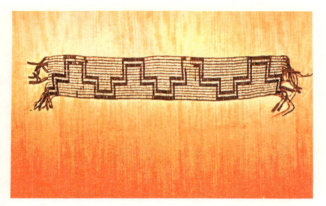

The Great God who is the power and wisdom that made you and me Incline your hearts to Righteousness Love and peace. This I send to assure you of my love, and to desire your Love to my friends, and when the Great God brings me among you I Intend to order all things in such manner that we may all live in Love and peace one with another whill I hope the Great God will Incline both me and you to do. I seek nothing but the honor of his name, and that we who are his workmanship, may do that whill is well pleasing to him. The man whill delivers this unto you, is my Special friend, Sober wise and Loving, you may believe him. I have already taken Care that none were of my people wrong you, by good Laws I have provided for that purpose, nor will I ever allow any of my people to sell Rumme to make your people Drunk. If anything should be out of order, expect when I come, it shall be mended, and I will bring you some things of our Country that are useful and pleasing to you. So I rest In ye Love of our god yt made us I am

England 25 : 2 : 1682

Your Loveing Freind

Wm Penn

I read this to the Indian by an Interpr: te the 6 mo 1682
Tho: Holme

37

ELEVEN TRIBES

Following are names of eleven of the main Plains Indian tribes:

ASSINIBOIN: In Chippewa this means "one who cooks by the use of stone," probably referring to stones that have been heated. The Assiniboin once belonged to the Sioux.

CHEYENNE: This comes from the Sioux term applied to people who speak a foreign tongue. The Cheyenne were in the Algonkin family and were all allies of the Sioux in the famous battle of the Little Bighorn.

ARAPAHO: The name comes from the Pawnee for "trader"; their Dakota name signifies "blue cloud."

APACHE: These Indians called themselves *Inde* or *Nde*, meaning "people." They were fierce warriors, so the Zuni called them *Ápachy*, "enemy."

GROS VENTRE ("Big Belly"): This tribe included the Hidatsa. The term also applied to the Atsina who lived on the Big Belly area of what is now Canada. Hidatsa spoke Sioux and were related to the Crow.

COMANCHE: These Indians lived entirely on the Great Plains. The Texas Rangers were established to deal with them.

DAKOTA ("Allies"), or SIOUX ("Vipers"): They were fine horsemen, the heroes or villains of many tales. Their chiefs include Sitting Bull, Red Cloud, and Crazy Horse.

BLACKFOOT, or SIKSIKA: These Indians were probably so-called because they dyed their moccasins black, perhaps with the ashes of prairie fires.

CROW: This is the English for *Absároke*, which means "bird men." They were most closely related to the Hidatsa.

SHOSHONE: The significance of this name is unknown. The Snake were a Shoshone tribe. One of their women, Sacajawea, made history guiding Lewis and Clark. They were unusually friendly toward whites.

SARSI, or SARCEE: This name comes from the Siksika words, *sa arsi*, meaning "not good." It is said that most of their medicine men were women.

WHAT'S IN A NAME?

Now you've heard the names of the tribes, but white men gave Plains Indians other names that were based on the way the Indians lived. For instance, they were called Horse Indians. Since they were not farmers, they had no permanent homes. As hunters they had to keep following the buffalo. Horses made this way of life easier and so they were known as Horse Indians. They were also called Buffalo Indians because they depended on buffalo for almost everything. Their clothes were made of its hide. So were the tipis in which they lived. From the bones they made needles and other tools. The list of things they made from buffalo would fill a page.

"But you told us only the names of the tribes. How did they name the babies? What did they call each other?"

As soon as a papoose was born, his family or the medicine man chose a name. Sometimes the name was picked because of something that happened. Chief Red Cloud got his name because on the day he was born, a cloud of red men, warriors, came over a nearby hill. Or a papoose might be named for an ancestor. The name was usually changed a bit. If his grandfather was Deer Horn, he might be Running Deer.

A warrior didn't always carry the same name for life. He could change it to

celebrate some heroic deed, or his friends might give him a new name. Perhaps he got hurt, and after that men called him Little Wound. For instance, one Sioux lad was named Jumping Badger because he was so quick to jump away from danger. Later, after he proved his skill at the hunt, he was called Four Horns. Finally he won the name Sitting Bull. With that name, he went down in history, the heroic. . . .

"What's heroic about a bull who just sits there?"

That's a good question. Let me show you how the meaning gets twisted when Indian names are changed to English. Sitting Bull's Indian name was Tatanka Yotanka. That means "warrior-solidly-planted-in-front-of-enemy-refusing-to-move." Can you imagine shouting

European voyagers explored the San Francisco bay area in the 17th century. The first settlement was founded in 1776 by the Spaniards, who later established a mission dedicated to Saint Francis of Assisi. The city of San Francisco grew up around this small nucleus.
Left: A photograph of the city as it appeared in 1856. Right: The huge steel Bay Bridge that connects the city with the suburb of Oakland. The bridge is more than 4½ miles long. The island of Yerba Buena, site of the original Franciscan mission, lies under its midpoint. Today San Francisco is a bustling city of almost 800,000 inhabitants. It's fine natural harbor is the largest port on the West Coast.

that in the heat of battle? So they called him Sitting Bull. Get it? You can see how shortening names can make quite a difference. Take Crazy Horse, another famous chief. You might think he was named after a horse that was not quite right in the head. Not at all. The Indian words mean "he-who-drives-the-horses-crazy-with-terror."

It is clear that Indians often used one word to say things that take many words in English. Some Indians had short names, like Eagle Ribs or Wolf Plume. Others come out very long in English, like Playing-Dead-Beside-the-Buffalo.

"You tell us only about warriors. Didn't Indian girls have names, too?"

Well, Lazy Boy gave his daughter a name that would remind everyone of his own horse-stealing raids. He called her Woman-Steals-Many-Horses, even though she had never taken a horse.

Bear Chief married a girl named Elk-Hollering-in-the-Water. Iron Horse's wife was Double-Victory-Calf-Robe. Maybe you can imagine how they happened to get their names.

"The names sound like stories, but they aren't very pretty. What girl wants people to think of her as an elk hollering in the water?"

But, Daisy, they had pretty names, too. Wouldn't you like to be called Morning Light, Silver Moon, Scented Flower, Bright-Colored Butterfly, or Little Bird? You wouldn't? You'd rather be Daisy?

Little Bird's Indian name was Sacajawea. She was the most famous Indian woman in the Far West. She was the guide for the first white men who ever crossed what is now the western United States.

Without her help, who knows if Lewis and Clark would ever have reached the Pacific Ocean alive? She knew the wild land of the Rockies like her own back yard. Now we come to her story.

41

A GREAT NATION IS BORN

Late in the 18th century, the United States became a free nation. Americans won their independence from England in the Revolutionary War (1775–81). The new nation stretched from the Atlantic Coast to the Mississippi. Beyond, the land was Spain's. Spain angered the American settlers by blocking their right to ship through New Orleans, Louisiana, at the mouth of the Mississippi. Then Spain ceded Louisiana to France. That meant that Napoleon became a neighbor, which didn't seem much of an improvement.

AN UNSEEN PURCHASE

The Ohio Valley settlers' only interest in Louisiana was that whoever owned it would let them ship their hogs and grain down the Mississippi and through the port of New Orleans. To most easterners, Louisiana meant nothing. But to Thomas Jefferson, third President of the United States, Louisiana meant a vast empire beyond the Mississippi. True, no one knew the exact boundaries of Louisiana. Jefferson liked to think it ran clear to the Pacific Ocean. Also, nobody knew what the country was like. It had never been completely explored. Some said it was just desert. Others thought a great inland waterway ran all the way across it. You could sail across America by boat!

Even though so little was known of the West, Jefferson dreamed of an America that ran "from sea to shining sea." His chance came in 1803, when Napoleon offered to sell Louisiana for $15,000,000.

"Sold!" said Jefferson, through his envoy James Monroe (a later president). Then, oh, what a howl went up from Congress! What, pay that huge sum when you didn't know what you were buying? Albert Gallatin, Secretary of the Treasury, was outraged. Was he supposed to hand over $15,000,000 for an unknown stretch of real estate, probably all sand and rattlesnakes? Remember, $15,000,000 at that time seemed more like $15,000,000,000 does today.

But Jefferson won the battle. Congress finally ratified the treaty for the Louisiana Purchase. Now all Jefferson had to do was to send out explorers to discover what kind of deal he'd made for his people.

Thomas Jefferson (1743–1826), one of the authors of the Declaration of Independence, served as third president of the United States. He successfully concluded the Louisiana Purchase, gaining control of a large territory from the French.

THE GREAT ADVENTURE BEGINS

Jefferson began planning to explore the West even before he bought it. He chose Captain Meriwether Lewis to command the great expedition. He knew the 29-year-old captain and trusted him, for Lewis was his secretary. Lewis was also a frontiersman who had fought under General "Mad Anthony" Wayne and battled Shawnee Indians. To help lead the expedition, Lewis chose a fellow soldier —William "Redhead" Clark. Clark was another veteran of Indian wars.

Jefferson gave Lewis quite a task. Lewis was ordered to seek the water route that was supposed to link the Atlantic and the Pacific. If it could be found, goods could be shipped across the country by water. Then ships could avoid the long voyage around the tip of South America.

But whether or not he found it, Lewis had to map a route across the country. First he was to follow the Missouri River to its source. Then he was to cross the Great Divide to the source of the Columbia River and follow it to the sea.

Sound easy? Well, men knew about the Missouri. They had found the mouth of the Columbia, on the Pacific Coast. But who knew what lay between these rivers? No one knew where the Great Divide was. They knew only that it was the spot where water running east flowed to the Gulf of Mexico, and water running west would reach the Pacific.

Besides filling in that big white blank on the map, Lewis had to make a report on the flowers, the animals, the climate. . . .

"Is that all?"

No, Daisy, there's more. And a very important part. He had to learn all he could about the people who lived there, the Indians. He had to tell them they were living under the rule of the United States. He was bringing them the news that the official government of the United States was now located in Washington, D.C. So they must be good, loyal, obedient. . . .

"Was that good news to the Indians?"

Not really. The hardest, most dangerous part of the job was to persuade Indians that they should be ruled by white men. (There is still conflict on this subject today.)

Near St. Louis, Lewis and Clark collected their men, boats, and supplies. They had three boats packed with flour, salt, guns, tools, and—most important—21 bales of gifts with which they hoped to create good feelings among the Indians.

On May 14, 1804, Lewis and Clark set off. They sailed up the Missouri with 43 men, two horses, and Lewis' big dog Scammon. The men were young and strong, good hunters and experienced woodsmen. One was the French trapper Drouillard, or Drewyer, expert on Indian sign language. He was to be the interpreter. Another, John Colter, was a bold adventurer who would later explore the Rockies. A third, Pierre Cruzatte, with one sightless eye and the other failing, was still a superb boatman and wonderful hunter.

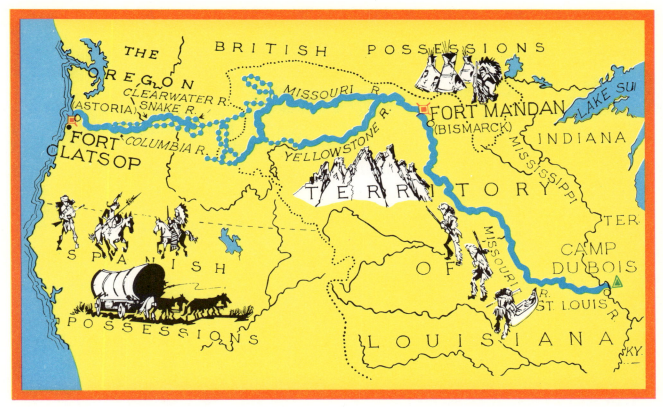

Opposite page: The city of St. Louis, at the junction of the Missouri and Mississippi rivers. Above: Map showing the route of the Lewis and Clark expedition from Camp Dubois to Fort Clatsop. The group set out on May 14, 1804, and returned on September 23, 1806. For 28 months about 40 men explored the Great Plains. The diaries of Lewis and Clark, published after their return, furnished important new information and paved the way for the settlement of the Far West.

And we mustn't forget the giant black man, York, Clark's servant. Besides his great strength he had other talents that helped the party through many tight spots. He had the gift of making people laugh. He charmed and delighted the Indians, who thought he was a super-human being.

OFF TO A GOOD START

The explorers first sailed west up the Missouri. Pouring rain, violent winds, and flash floods almost drove the boats crashing against the riverbanks or into islands. The crews worked frantically and kept the boats afloat. Some men jumped off and, wading knee-deep in mud, towed the boats with ropes. Even in calm weather,

there were dangers—tree trunks sticking out of the water, sandbars, tricky currents. And there were snakes, leeches, and swarms of mosquitoes. But this was the easy part of the trip.

They turned north at the point where the Kansas River joined the Missouri. By July 21, they reached the mouth of the Platte. Knowing there were Oto Indians around, they called a meeting at a place they named Council Bluff. The response was poor: 13 Indians came and only 6 of them were chiefs. Still, it was an important event, for this was the first official contact between the United States and its new subjects.

Acting as ambassador, Lewis gave certificates from the President to three chiefs. The certificates meant the government

45

viewed them as heads of their tribes. Lewis told them their new rulers wanted them to stop raiding other tribes and to make peace. Then he handed out the presents —medals and bottles of whiskey.

The Oto didn't like their presents. They sulked and grumbled that the Great White Father was very stingy. A few days later, one Oto chief grandly handed back his certificate. By doing this he hoped to frighten the white men and make them lose face.

It didn't work. Lewis scolded him severely. When the chief's friend asked if he could have the certificate, Lewis refused. The word went out among the tribes of the river: you can't scare these men!

BLACKBIRD'S MAGIC SPELL

Lewis and Clark expected to meet the Omaha above the mouth of the Little Sioux River. The Omaha Indians had been the terror of the fur traders before the smallpox epidemic of 1802. But so many died in that epidemic that the Omaha lost power. The most terrible blow of all was the death of their fierce Chief Blackbird from smallpox.

In his day, Blackbird was the worst pirate in the whole region. A swaggering bully, he set up a reign of terror along the river. He took anything he wanted from the fur traders. No one dared to stop him. He even took guns and bullets for his braves. The braves usually returned the bullets—right into a trapper's body— in the next raid.

Blackbird was crafty, too. He made more trouble by telling the Ponca that the traders were plotting to kill them. The Ponca promptly went on the warpath.

Blackbird boasted that his spirits had given him "powerful medicine"—a magic spell. With his spell, he could kill anyone he didn't like. First he predicted the man's

Scenes and figures of the Far West were favorite subjects of many 19th-century American artists. In this painting by Frederic Remington, one of the best-known of the artists, an Indian guide scans the snow-covered prairies.

Above: A Mandan Indian village, painted by George Catlin. Catlin gave up his law practice and spent several years living among the Indians. Many of his drawings and paintings now hang in the Smithsonian Institution in Washington, D.C.

death. Then the prediction came true with amazing speed. There was a story that he gave a feast for 60 men and every brave was dead by morning!

Blackbird really did have some "powerful medicine." It was the poison arsenic, sold to him by some white men. He used it generously to make everyone think that his spirits would strike anyone he hated.

When Blackbird died, no one was sorry but the Omaha. They gave him a grand funeral. He was buried with his war-horse, war paints, weapons, and ornaments. On his grave they planted a cedar tree. His burial mound was high on a hill overlooking the Missouri, so he could watch the white men sailing up the river.

If he could have watched Lewis and Clark coming up the river, he would have been very angry. The explorers knew the Omaha were around, but they were not afraid. No one was, with Blackbird gone.

These white men were so bold as to visit Blackbird's grave and even walk over his burial mound!

LAND OF THE SIOUX

In late August the explorers passed the Big Sioux River. Here, the Indians said, there were "devils" 18 inches high, but

they were not to be seen. The first Sioux tribe whom the white men met were the Yankton. They were friendly. First they danced, and then York danced for them. The white men then showed off by firing the newly invented air rifle.

But trouble was coming. In September, near the Teton River, three Indian boys swam out to the boats. Nearby lay 140 tipis of their people, they said. This was bad news, for their people were the ferocious Teton Sioux. Worse yet, the Teton showed how little they thought of the white men by sending mere boys to greet them.

Battle alert! That night, only a third of the men slept on shore. The rest stayed on the boats, ready for action. Their guns were cocked, and three swivel catapults loaded with scrap iron were aimed at the shore.

Above: A Mandan Indian brave in a portrait by Karl Bodmer. The young Indian holds a flute that he used to serenade his beloved.
Below, left: Herds of cattle grazing in the Rocky Mountains. The melting snows feed the waters of the Bighorn River in the foreground.

The next day the Teton arrived—60 braves led by Black Buffalo and The Partisan. These chiefs had attacked many trappers before. The Partisan was known far and wide as one of the meanest bullies on the river. There were stories that when one young Indian girl refused to become his squaw, he promptly shot her dead.

Now Jefferson's envoys would be tested. At last they were face to face with the tribe that ruled the river.

BOLDNESS CONQUERS

Lewis first tried to be friendly. He greeted the chiefs and began handing out presents: red coats, cocked hats, feathers, tobacco. Black Buffalo did not say "Thank you." He said "More."

The chiefs made severe demands: Lewis must give them one whole boat com-

Above: Another portrait of an Indian brave, this one by A. J. Miller. The young hunter's hair style and the decorations on his clothes tell us that he belongs to the Chinook.
Below, right: The dense forest at the foot of the mountains was Indian hunting territory.

In this painting an American artist portrayed his version of the meeting between Lewis and Clark and the Flathead Indians. The historic meeting took place in what is now Montana.

pletely equipped. If not, they would not let the white men go up the river.

Lewis asked the two chiefs and three of the braves to come on board for a drink. The Indians gulped down the whiskey, but it did not warm their hearts. Lewis showed off the air rifle. It didn't scare them.

"All right, off the boat," Clark ordered the Indians. He began hustling the braves ashore. They saw their threat had failed. The Partisan, pretending to be drunk, fell against Clark and tried to knock him down. Clark pulled his sword.

It was a tense moment. The Teton were looking into 3 catapults and 30 rifles, aimed directly at them.

Black Buffalo gave in and began to bargain. Wouldn't the white men give him some clothes for his squaws? Couldn't he go back onto the white men's boat?

Clark took the chief and several other braves back on board for the night. He felt it was safer to have them in a place where he could keep an eye on them.

Four tense days of threat and counter-threat followed. Then the Sioux backed down. Just give them some tobacco, they said, and they would let the white men go up the river after all.

The news spread like wildfire: these white men had tamed the Sioux!

A MAN OF SPIRIT

News of the victory reached the next village well ahead of the boats. It was a village of a tribe known as the Arikara; they gave the white men a royal welcome. The white heroes had come to the right place for a good time. The tribe offered them feasting, dancing, and friendly Indian girls eager to entertain visitors. And of course the boats could go up the river. Who would dare to stop them now?

Clark wrote in his diary that these Indians were dirty, kind, poor, and extravagant. Everyone thought they were the most charming Indians you could meet. But a certain fur trader, whose goods the

with wild applause. What a prize catch he would be as a husband! Indian girls clustered around him, each hoping to charm him into marrying her.

York was tired but he did the best he could to entertain the Arikara. But winter was coming, Clark was sick, and it was time to build a winter camp. So the black "goodwill ambassador" moved on with the boats to the villages of the Mandan Indians. In a poplar wood nearby the men built Fort Mandan. Today Bismarck, North Dakota, stands on the spot where Lewis and Clark spent the winter.

INTRODUCING SACAJAWEA

The explorers had never seen such cold, snowy weather. But the fort was snug and there was plenty to eat. One hunt brought in "34 deer, 10 elk, 5 buffalo." The Indians stayed around the fort, bringing corn and squash to trade for beads

Arikara had taken 2 months before, might not have agreed.

If the Arikara now liked white men, a black man made even more of a hit with them. They crowded around York, looking at his skin, making noises of wonder and amazement. Was that his real color? Would it wash off? Children tagged at his heels wherever he went. If he turned and roared at them in fun, they ran off screaming. His singing and dancing were greeted

and other trinkets. At night by a roaring fire, Cruzatte played his fiddle for square dancing. Soldiers with bandanas tied to their arms were "girl" partners.

Lewis never forgot that he was an ambassador as well as an explorer. He spent much of the winter working out an agreement among Mandan, Arikara, and Gros Ventre. They promised to form an alliance against the Teton Sioux. Lewis said Washington would help them. Three years later, the Arikara became more dangerous river pirates than the Sioux had been.

One visitor was Toussaint Charbonneau, who lived with the Gros Ventre and knew their language. He wanted a job as interpreter. Lewis hired him. This was a great stroke of luck, for Toussaint brought along his two Indian wives. And the younger wife was Sacajawea.

"Hooray! Another girl in the story!"

Yes, Daisy. And Sacajawea—or "Bird Woman," as she is called in English—was one of the great heroines of the West.

STORY OF A HEROINE

Sacajawea was the daughter of a Snake Indian chief. When she was only 10, the Gros Ventre attacked her tribe. The braves scattered to escape a massacre. Most of them got away on horseback. But the raiders caught Sacajawea while she was trying to wade the river. For 5 years they held her as a slave and treated her brutally.

Now grown up, she caught Charbonneau's eye. He could use another strong young squaw, and this was a pretty one. He won her from her owner in a gambling game. But she was no better off than before, for Charbonneau too treated her like a slave.

Sacajawa was 16 when she came to the fort. Here she found herself in a new world. The Americans were kind to her! Most of her life, she had been beaten and mistreated. She was so grateful for their kindness that she worshiped the Americans, especially the "Redheaded Chief," Clark.

Clark grew fond of the Indian girl. He saw that she would soon have a baby, yet Charbonneau was still unkind to her. This so angered Clark that he threatened to kill Charbonneau if he continued to mistreat his pregnant wife.

"Did she have the baby?"

Yes, she had a son in February. She called him Jean-Baptiste, or Pomp. Lewis gave Sacajawea powdered rattlesnake rattles to ease her labor pains.

"Ugh, that couldn't help!"

Daisy is right, but the explorers didn't know much about medicine.

In April, 1805, they started off into the unknown. They sent a boat back to St. Louis laden with specimens of flowers, plants, and minerals. After that, nothing was heard from them for over a year. In

Three great Indian chiefs in a portrait by Paul Kane, a Canadian artist who painted North American Indians. Left to right: A Blackfoot, a Sarsi, and a Blood. Many of Kane's paintings hang in the Parliament buildings in Ottawa, Canada.

June they reached the Great Falls of the Missouri, where the Rockies begin. They had to carry boats and goods around the falls.

Over and over, Sacajawea proved her worth to the expedition. She found edible roots, sewed moccasins, helped save a boat. With her papoose on her back, she scouted the riverbank for familiar landmarks. To her joy, she began recognizing peaks and rock formations that told her she was coming home. Eagerly she ran ahead, guiding the expedition to the land of the Snake.

2,800 MILES FROM ST. LOUIS

On July 15, after a trip of nearly 2,800 miles, the explorers reached the source of the Missouri, Three Forks. Sacajawea was wildly excited. This was the very spot where raiders had attacked her tribe and kidnaped her!

Here three streams joined. The one they named Jefferson looked like the best route. Inching over its wild, rock-choked waters, they realized that no ship could cross America. Quietly the dream of the "inland waterway" died.

It was not easy to meet the Snake.

53

A meeting between Cree and Blackfoot Indians. The meeting took place in about 1850 in northern Montana. The chiefs raised their arms to show that the meeting would be a peaceful one. The Cree had come from Canada to barter.

These Indians knew nothing of white men, and mistook the explorers for their enemies, the fierce Blackfoot. They fled in terror. At last Lewis caught up with a chief and a band of braves. He lured them to camp by promising to give them presents and show them marvels: a man with a black skin and a girl of their own tribe.

Cautiously the Snake approached the camp. Sacajawea came out. With a wild yell, she ran to the chief and threw her arms around him. Casting her blanket over him, sucking her fingers (Indian for "my people"), weeping with joy, she told the amazed men: "This is my brother!" Now she who had been a slave came back to her rightful place as sister of the chief. As such, she was able to persuade her tribe to help the white men who had been so kind to her. The Snake gave the men horses and led them through Lemhi Pass, which is on what is now the Montana-Idaho border. Here they crossed the Great Divide. A salmon in the stream was proof. These waters ran west to the Columbia and so to the Pacific Ocean.

THE MOST TERRIBLE MOUNTAINS

The explorers were on the Salmon River, which ran to the Snake, thence to

the Columbia. But only a salmon could travel that rocky gorge, edged by cliffs. The Snake told Lewis all they had learned about the area from the Nez Percé, a tribe Lewis had never heard of before. Lewis asked an old Indian scout, Toby, how the Nez Percé managed to cross the mountains. By a bad road, Toby said. Men could starve on that road, or freeze, for it was late August and already cold. The white men had better winter here, with the Snake.

Lewis refused. He had to get to the sea before winter. Where Indians went, his men could go. He hired Toby as a guide, and they set out. The "bad road" was worse than Toby had said. They climbed through snow and sleet. Horses fell over cliffs and slid down icy rocks. Men gasped for breath in the high altitude. Their moccasins froze to their feet. Living on a few roots, berries, and dried salmon, they suffered from constant hunger. At least the Indians were friendly—Nez Percé, Yakima, Flathead, and later Walla Walla and Chinook. Seeing Sacajawea in the party, the Indians knew these white men came in peace. The Nez Percé generously shared their food, although some of the roots made the white men very sick.

They struggled painfully across what one called "the most terrible mountains ever seen." Through the tricky Lolo Pass,

down the Clearwater to the Snake, down the Snake, and finally down the Columbia they went. At last, on November 7, Clark could write in his journal: "Ocean in view! O! the joy!"

THE MISERABLE WINTER

But the ocean was not "in view." The shore was still some miles away. What Clark saw were huge sea waves rolling in from the west up the 12-mile-wide Columbia. The little canoes bobbed like corks, and Sacajawea became seasick.

And the "joy" didn't last. Rain fell in torrents. Gales roared in from the Pacific, and the tides almost swamped the boats. The local Indians seemed somewhat untrustworthy. They had met white men before, and had ways of dealing with them.

Lewis gave up the idea of camping on the coast. His men built Fort Clatsop on

At left: A camp of Shoshone Indians in the Wyoming Mountains. The Shoshone were divided into groups. Those living in the East belonged to the tribes of the Great Plains. Those in the South were nomads who roamed the desert. Above: Washakie, one of the most powerful chiefs of the Eastern Shoshone, was a friend of the white man. An old Shoshone legend relates that when Washakie reached the age of 70, the young men of his tribe, judging him too old to fight, relieved him of his command. He disappeared and returned 2 months later with 6 scalps take from enemies on the warpath. Needless to say, his command was restored.

high ground some miles from the shore. Clark, York, and some others went to the beach to dip a finger in the Pacific, so they could say they'd touched the sea.

At Fort Clatsop the men spent a miserable winter. Rain fell constantly. Gales reached hurricane force. Only 12 days were free of rain; only 6 were sunny. Clothes and blankets were covered with mildew and began to rot. No one was ever really dry or warm. Their only game was elk, and its meat was lean and tough. They had no whiskey to warm their shivering bodies. Even tobacco was so scarce they had to save it for trade on the return trip.

Lewis studied the maps they had made and planned the return. He and Clark realized they probably had not found the best and shortest route. In March they started back. In many places the way was still blocked by snow. The party divided at Three Forks, so that Lewis could explore one route, and Clark another. They joined again and compared notes. At the Mandan villages they said goodbye to Sacajawea and Pomp.

"What happened to them?"

Well, Clark wrote, asking them to move to St. Louis so Pomp could go to school. History books tell of an elderly squaw named Sacajawea who died sometime during the 1800's, and perhaps that was our heroine. But I'd rather remember a young girl running through the forest with her papoose on her back, showing men the way through the Rockies.

THE END OF THE MIRACLE

On September 23, 1806, a group of weary men straggled into St. Louis. Worn-out by hardship, dressed in smelly rags patched together with buffalo tendons, they were a wild-looking lot. People backed away from them, whispering, wondering who these ragged, hairy strangers could be.

When people found out this was the Lewis and Clark expedition returned home, they were filled with disbelief. Everyone thought they were dead, lost in the wilderness or massacred by Indians. The news spread like wildfire: a miracle! They had made it.

It was indeed a miracle. They were the first Americans to cross the continent from the Mississippi to the mouth of the Columbia. For over 2 years they had traveled 9,000 miles through trackless wilds, over soaring mountains, along impassable streams. They had brought back priceless information about the unknown Far West. They had mapped routes for future explorers, and had given the United States a claim to the Oregon country.

On a big pine near a stream called the Lewis and Clark River, these words are carved: "Wm. Clark, December 3rd 1805 By Land from the U. States in 1804 & 5."

When Clark stood in the rain and dug those words into the bark, he said it all. America claimed the West.

HOW LEGENDS
ARE BORN

Have you ever played "gossip"? You whisper a message to the person beside you, and he whispers it to the next one. When the message gets to the end of the line, it isn't what you said at all!

That is what often happened to news in the old West. News was seldom written down. Usually it spread by one person's telling another. With no television, newspapers, or books, western men amused themselves by telling tall tales around the campfire. The truth is, they *did* have wild adventures. But they loved to boast and make the story still bigger. If a man wounded an Indian he might say he had killed him. Later perhaps he'd say he'd killed five. By the time the story got to the next camp, men were saying he had beaten a whole war party all by himself!

Gossip about real deeds turned real men into heroes of legends. Other heroes, like Paul Bunyan, never actually existed. They were made up just for fun by the storytellers around the campfire.

PAUL BUNYAN AND OTHER HEROES

In the forests of the Northwest, the storytellers said, lived a giant logger, Paul Bunyan. He had a blue ox named Babe who could drink a river dry. When he swung his ax around his head, he cut down every tree for miles.

Once a winding river squirted gallons of water in Paul's beard, and then threw turtles and muskrats at him. This made Paul very angry. He trapped some blizzards and used them to freeze the river. Then he hitched Babe up to the river, and Babe yanked that river straight!

Paul created Puget Sound and the Grand Canyon by digging them out with his two bare hands. Work like that made him hungry. He was such a huge eater that he had a special pan, big enough to make enough pancakes for him. The pan was so big that Paul greased it by tying two pieces of lard to an ordinary man's feet. Then the man skated around in the pan.

"But cowboys who lived where there were hardly any trees wouldn't care anything about a giant lumberjack."

Well, Daisy, how about Pecos Bill, the hero of the Southwest? Bill was so tough he used a live rattlesnake for a lasso. Once he hugged two grizzly bears to death. When a dry spell hit Texas, Bill rode to Oklahoma, roped a huge cloud, and

Opposite page: A scene from Walt Disney's comic interpretation of the adventures of the fearless Texan Pecos Bill. With Bill is his friend Sluefoot Sue.

Above: The lonely landscape of an area of the Painted Desert in northern Arizona.
Right: This rich green forest lies on the banks of Yellowstone Lake in the southern part of Yellowstone National Park. Fed by rivers and mountain streams, the waters of the lake teem with fish. These two photographs are examples of the many varied landscapes of the western portions of the United States.

pulled it home. The cloud rained so much, the water made the Rio Grande and the Gulf of Mexico.

There was nothing Bill couldn't ride, but one time he did get thrown That was when he rode the cyclone. The cyclone

bucked and twisted and knocked down mountains. Bill hung on. Then the tricky cyclone rained itself out from under him. Bill landed so hard he dug out Death Valley!

The boatmen had a hero too: Mike Fink. Unlike Paul Bunyan and Pecos Bill, Mike was a real person. Men who toiled all day poling boats up rivers had to be tough, and Mike was the toughest. He said that as a baby, he had turned down milk and yelled for whiskey. He'd stand on his boat and yell that he could beat anybody in a race, a shooting match, or drinking bout. Usually he could. He could drive a nail with a single shot, or shoot a tin cup off a man's head.

This risky game, plus a hot temper, was the ruin of Mike. He quarreled with his best friend, Carpenter, about a girl. Later they made up. Or did they? They got drunk together, and Mike said they

63

should play the game to prove they were friends. Carpenter put the cup of whiskey on his head. Mike took aim and fired. Carpenter fell to the ground, shot through the forehead.

Knowing what a good shot Mike was, nobody would believe it was an accident. Talbot, the gunsmith, openly accused Mike of murder. When Mike came to camp to face his accuser and put an end to the talk, Talbot shot Mike dead.

"Did that really happen?"

Well, Mike really lived and some of it happened.

"How about things that *really* happened?"

All right, Daisy, next I'll tell you about John Colter. His story really happened, but people thought he made it up. And the story got bigger in the telling.

"COLTER'S HELL"

Once people thought hell was a place under the ground, a land of fire, smoke, and steam that smelled of sulfur. So . . .

"I thought you were going to tell about John Colter."

trails and animal tracks 500 miles through the wilds of Wyoming. And he brought back more than beaver skins. He brought enough tales of wonders to keep the camps buzzing for years.

He told of a land of boiling, bubbling fountains. Steam jets spurted hundreds of feet into the air. Clouds of steam smelling like sulfur poured out of holes in the ground. There were lakes where you could get trout already boiled.

"You call that facts? Nobody fishes for boiled trout!"

Well, that part was made up. But in his lake you really could boil a trout that you had caught.

"I think he made it all up."

Well, Daisy, lots of other people thought so too. They laughed and asked him, "Do you think you have discovered hell?" For a joke they named that land "Colter's Hell."

Steamboats like the one pictured here sill ply the waters of the Mississippi River. Their flat keels and paddle wheels allow them to sail in shallow waters.

I'm coming to him. As a young explorer he proved his skill and courage with Lewis and Clark. His pay was about $5 a month. He saw the wealth of beaver in the streams, and was tempted. A man could make a lot of "beaver dollars" here: Money could be earned by trapping beavers and selling their skins. So on the return trip Colter left the group of explorers at the Mandan villages and struck off into the wilderness.

For months he struggled over mountains and down steep gorges no white man had ever seen before. He followed Indian

But the joke would be on you, Daisy, and on the people who laughed. Would you like to visit his "hell" and see for yourself? Today it is a national park, visited by millions of people. For Colter was talking about the geysers and boiling mud pots of Yellowstone National Park.

A RACE FOR LIFE

In 1807 a fur trader named Manuel Lisa set up Fort Lisa in Montana where the Bighorn and Yellowstone rivers join. He hired Colter to make friends with the Blackfoot and get them to trade beaver skins for trinkets. Colter went back to the wilderness. But he got into many fights with the Blackfoot, and killed a number of their braves. Because of this, they swore revenge against him.

Soon their chance came. Hiding among the trees, the Blackfoot saw Colter and another trapper, John Potts, paddling a canoe upstream. The Indians closed in, and suddenly Colter and Potts were surrounded by 800 fierce warriors.

The Indians killed Potts at once, but they caught Colter alive. They had a special plan for him. They stripped off all his clothes and told him he could go free if he could win a race against their fastest braves. They even gave him a head start of a few hundred feet.

At the signal, Colter was off like an arrow. Close behind him ran the braves, waving spears, each wanting to be the first to catch him and kill him. Colter dashed barefoot over sharp stones and cactus that cut his feet. His torn feet left a trail of blood. But he kept running at top speed for 6 miles. By that time his nose was bleeding, too.

All but one of his pursuers had fallen behind, worn out. One Indian still pounded close at his heels, thrusting out a spear to stab the white man. Like lightning, Colter whipped around, seized the spear, and plunged it into the Indian.

Gasping but not daring to rest, Colter took off again. He reached the Madison River, plunged in, and swam to a floating clump of tree branches. There he hid all day, with just the tip of his nose out of water so he could breathe. The angry Blackfoot hunted everywhere, but they could not find him.

By nightfall the Indians were gone. But Colter did not dare go down the river. There might be guards watching for him where its gorge joined the canyon. So he climbed straight up the cliff. He hauled himself up by seizing bushes and hanging on to ledges. By dawn he reached the top of the mountain and, worn-out, fell in the snow to rest.

The Princess *was one of the most famous steam-boats to sail the Mississippi. These boats, pouring smoke and flame from their tall smokestacks, were perhaps the most romantic and picturesque part of the landscape of the great river.*

He was 300 miles from Fort Lisa. He had no clothes, no weapons but the spear, and nothing to eat but roots and tree bark. He started walking. After 7 days and nights he reached the fort. As he came in, he was almost shot by a watchman who took him for a "strange animal." Can you picture what he looked like by then?

"I don't believe anyone could do it!"

At first the other trappers didn't believe him either, Daisy. Luckily he had the Indian's spear for proof. Besides, why would he go around naked, with bleeding feet, unless it all happened just as he had described?

So Colter won his race for life. But the

67

terrible strain and hard life of a Rocky Mountain trapper took a great deal out of him. Colter was worn-out and sick by the time he was 40. He returned to Missouri, where he died in 1813. He was buried on Tunnel Hill, so called because the Missouri-Pacific Railroad ran through it. Later workers dug up the cemetery, and his grave was lost. But Colter's race is remembered.

JIM BRIDGER'S ARROW

The men who accompanied Lewis and Clark spread the word that the mountain streams were full of beaver. Beaver skins brought a high price because beaver hats were fashionable. The race for furs began. In 1822, William Ashley, a fur trader, formed a new kind of fur company. Instead of trading with Indians for furs, his men went into the wilds and trapped beaver themselves.

Among the group were some of America's greatest scouts and explorers: Jedediah Smith, Thomas Fitzpatrick, and Jim Bridger. The forts they built—Fort Laramie, Fort Hall, Fort Bent, Fort Bridger—were welcome rest spots for later wagon trains. And in their search for beaver, they blazed trails that pioneers would follow, such as sections of the Oregon, California, and Mormon trails.

For 50 years Jim Bridger ranged the Rockies. Often he clashed with Indians and was lucky to escape with the hair still on his head. Once some Blackfoot ambushed him and shot two arrows into his back before he could get away. One came out, but the other arrowhead stayed in his flesh for 3 years. To those who feared the wound might become infected, Bridger coolly said, "Meat never goes bad

in the mountains!" In 1835, Dr. Marcus Whitman, the Oregon pioneer, cut the arrowhead out with his hunting knife.

A man of steel, wouldn't you say? Bridger was the first white man to see the

John Colter, a trapper and guide, was probably the first white man to see the wonders of Yellowstone National Park. The famous Yellowstone geysers erupt at regular intervals, sometimes sending jets of steam over 100 feet into the air. Many of the geysers in Yellowstone National Park erupt with such regularity that their activity can be recorded on timetables. Old Faithful, one of the most famous geysers, provides a 4-minute display about every 65 minutes. Geysers are fascinating natural phenomena. Under each one is a channel leading to masses of hot rock. Underground water, heated by the rock, sometimes gets so hot that it turns to steam, which takes up much more space. When most of the water in the channel becomes steam, it erupts through the earth's surface.

Great Salt Lake. Some miles east of it he built his fort, an important stopping place on the Oregon Trail. With other trappers he helped blaze that trail. When the fur trade declined around 1840, he served as a government scout. Like other mountain men, he guided many wagon trains of pioneers on their way to settle the West.

THE MOUNTAIN MEN

The "free traders" of William Ashley's Rocky Mountain Fur Company were men of a new breed. In the past, Indians had trapped beaver and brought skins to the white man's forts to trade. Now this new kind of white man was out to beat the Indian trapper at his own game. To accomplish this, the mountain man had to live like an Indian.

He remained in the wilderness all year long. He never came back to civilization if he could help it. He stayed calm in the presence of hostile Indians, but cities made him nervous. His backyard was the rocky gorge, the raging mountain stream, the icy peak. Home was a tipi with an Indian wife mending moccasins and cooking deer meat on a campfire. (Women of Sacajawea's tribe, the Snake, were the prize beauties.) Sometimes a mountain man had to pay many beaver skins, even a horse, to buy a pretty squaw from her father. After that her whole family called the mountain man kin, and camped in his tipi whenever they felt like it.

The mountain man was tough and lean. He never shaved. His long hair fell loose around his shoulders. From the belt at his waist hung pistol, hatchet, knife, and gunpowder flask. It may sound odd, but this "man of steel" carried a purse! It dangled from his neck and held tobacco, a pipe, a tinderbox, bullets, a little dried meat. He

Forts such as those pictured at the right and below were originally built by explorers and traders and later by the Army. They were used as protection in time of attack. They also served as trading posts. Friendly Indians brought their arts, crafts, and hunting catches to the forts to exchange them for the necessities the white man could provide. Hunters and trappers, using the forts as a base, provided beaver and muskrat skins for the clothes of the fashionable ladies and gentlemen of the time. The elegant young man at the right wears a hat made of the hair of the beaver.

71

Mountain men (opposite page and above) were typical of the frontier. Living on the edges of civilization, these rough hunters contributed greatly to western expansion.

carried with him anything he might need on his long days and nights alone. Always present were his gun and traps.

He wore clothes of skins, decorated with porcupine quills and leather fringe. On his feet were beaded moccasins made by his squaw. His fur hat had a beaver tail or a horsehair braid in back.

"Quite a costume!"

Yes, Daisy, indeed it was. But to him they were work clothes. And he never took them off, unless the bugs bit too badly. Then he might drape his clothes over an anthill, so that the ants could devour the bugs.

MEN OF STEEL

The men of the mountains were free souls. They lived by their own code and cared nothing for ordinary laws. Sometimes, as one of the explorers, Hugh Glass, found out, they didn't even keep the code of the wilderness.

Once, while out trapping, Hugh was attacked by a huge grizzly bear. The bear almost tore him to ribbons. His horrified companions tried to dress his wounds, but they doubted that Hugh could live. They waited for him to die so they could bury him. But Hugh was in no hurry to die, and the trappers got restless. Two of them, John Fitzgerald and a young boy, agreed to stay behind with the dying man until the end. The rest of the party left.

A few days later the burial party caught up with the others. Fitzgerald had Hugh's rifle. It was all over, he said. Poor Hugh was dead and buried.

But Hugh was *not* dead. Only partly conscious, he had watched the men divide up his possessions. He swore he would not die until he had a chance to get even.

He crawled to a spring. Nearby grew wild cherries that he could pick. Incredibly, his wounds healed. Finally he dragged himself downstream and began the trip through hundreds of miles of wilderness. He was armed only with a razor blade.

When he reached camp, the men thought they were seeing a ghost. But no ghost ever had such a look of grim purpose.

At last he cornered Fitzgerald, who trembled before Hugh's glaring eyes. But Hugh did not strike. He simply reached out, took back his gun, and said, "You know what you did to me. Settle the matter with your conscience and your God."

DANGER EVERYWHERE

Grizzlies, rattlesnakes, hostile Indians lying in ambush—was that all the mountain men had to face?

Not at all. They pitted their lives against nature itself, and nature was fickle in the Rocky Mountains.

Hugh Glass was lucky enough to find wild fruit and perhaps a buffalo calf weak enough to be killed with a razor. But hunger was a constant threat to these tough men. In northern woods they found game and streams for drinking water. But fur-

Above, top: Trader Jim Bridger, one of the most famous mountain men, is credited with the discovery of Great Salt Lake. Pictured below him is Kit Carson. A colonel in the war with the Navajo, Carson married an Indian and often sided with the red man. Opposite: Sunset on the Painted Desert.

ther south, especially in summer, rocky deserts stretched, as barren as the moon.

Where the sun blazed down and not a green leaf could be seen for miles, they were lucky to dine on ants, grasshoppers, or snakes. They might have to eat the ears of their mules, or even roast their leather moccasins for supper. Some, sick from thirst, survived only by drinking their horses' blood.

"Ugh, how could anyone eat or drink such stuff?"

Well, maybe we all could, if it was either that or die! But nature could smile, too. What feasts they had in spring, when the buffalo returned to the mountains! Then they stuffed themselves—for tomorrow they might be starving again.

ROCKY MOUNTAIN FAIR

Do you remember how William Ashley changed fur trading when he turned the mountain men loose in the wilderness? But he did more than that. He worked out a way to make sure that they never had to come out of the wilderness at all.

"Then how would they trade their furs?"

He had a simple plan: Every year he sent the trading post to them. Yes, a trading post on horseback—a great caravan from St. Louis all the way to Henry's Fork of the Green River, almost as far west as Salt Lake.

The first "rendezvous," as they called it, was in June, 1825. From the east came the train of pack horses, plodding into the quiet mountain valley. From all over the Rockies, trappers came riding—800 braves with their squaws and children, 100 mountain men, and Spanish traders from Santa Fe. Believe me, that valley wasn't quiet any more!

All winter the men had trapped alone, with no company but their wives and other Indians. Now here they came, rich with beaver skins, eager to spend their year's work on a wild, roaring party. Pleasure first: plenty of whiskey, shooting matches, foot and horse races, wrestling, and gambling with the stakes rifles, horses, and even wives.

Those St. Louis traders knew what they were doing. By the time the whiskey barrels were empty, they had most of the

beaver skins. The mountain men then traded what they had left for coffee, sugar, weapons, horses, and other necessities. Or they listened to the pleas of their squaws for "foofaraw"—finery. A mountain man liked to think, "Nobody else's squaw is going to outshine *my* wife." So he traded his furs for beads, bells, rings, fancy hats, bright scarlet cloth—whatver his wife thought she just had to have to stay in style.

That first Rocky Mountain Fair brought the fur company $75,000 worth of beaver skins. For some years profits went up, bringing a fortune in furs. But during the 1830's other fur companies gave the Rocky Mountain Fur Company sharp competition. By 1840 the streams were trapped out, the beaver gone. The day of the mountain men was ending.

But in the 20 years of their glory, they had built forts, mapped trails, and opened the gates of the West. They had also changed the lives of the Indians. The white men had brought the trade goods that the Indians now craved, and the small-pox that killed thousands of Indians.

JUST FOR LAUGHS

Thanks to the mountain men, Americans were hearing facts about the West, as well as legends. They were also getting plenty of lies from the liars' bench. A "liars' bench" meant any group of men sitting around seeing who could tell the biggest whopper. Here are some:

Texas soil was so rich that if you planted a pack of needles, you could harvest a pile of steel bars. Texas grapes were sold one at a time—they were the size of melons. Grapefruits were so big that it took only six of them to make a dozen. You needed fox traps to catch Texas mosquitoes. The flies grew so big that Texas passed a law: All flies had to wear muzzles and dog tags. A Texas flea got so rich he could afford to hire his own dog.

Missouri River steamboats didn't need a river. They would run on a light dew. One time a pilot got drunk and ran the boat 8 miles up a dry creek.

Out on the Plains, the rattlesnakes were pretty poisonous. If one of them struck part of the wagon, the wood would start to swell. You'd have to cut away the piece of wood the rattler bit, in order to save the wagon's life.

Out in the West, the old-timer said, the soil was mighty rich. Pumpkin vines grew so fast they dragged pumpkins along the ground and bruised them. One day the old-timer sowed some cucumber seeds. He was tired, so he lay down for a nap. When he woke up, the cucumber vines had grown all around him and tied him to a tree! He had to take his knife and do some mighty fast cutting.

They had some pretty sharp winds in the West, too. During a Wyoming windstorm, a man said, he saw a Chinese fellow flying a kite. The kite was an iron shutter with a log chain for a tail. Another wind blew a cookstove 80 miles and came back the next day for the griddle.

The men who told these tales usually drank plenty of whiskey. It helped them think up whoppers. They called the whiskey "mule kick" or "tarantula juice." It was so strong it would kill a rattler who bit anyone that had been drinking it! Or so they said.

The song "Oh, Susanna" might be called the prospectors' hymn. The banjo mentioned was actually the pan used to filter sand that contained the gold.

THE HAPPY LAND

America was settled by people who were looking for "paradise on earth." The Spanish came for gold. Ponce de León sought the Fountain of Youth. The Puritans came to find freedom of worship. And pioneers kept pushing West looking for freedom, adventure, fortune—paradise.

When stories about California began to drift back east, many thought that the Happy Land had been found at last. Everything was bigger than life in California. Once a herd of cattle got lost in a hollowed-out redwood tree. Also, the climate was so health-giving that the only way to start a graveyard was to shoot somebody. If a man got sick with malaria, it was such a rare sight that people walked 18 miles to see him shiver. Then there was the Californian who moved to another state when he was 250 years old. He died, and they sent him back to California for burial. But as soon as he got into that wonderful air, he sprang back to life!

"Did people believe these things?"

No, but they did believe they could

Death Valley, California, shown above, is sometimes called the Devil's Wheatfield. Beneath the shining sun its bushes sometimes look like fields of grain. Actually, this is poor farming land, and the Indians who lived in this part of the country were forced to live on a diet of roots, insects, and whatever game they were occasionally able to find and kill.

make their fortunes in the West. They did believe it was a "land of milk and honey" ready for anyone who wanted it.

"Was that fact or nonsense?"

Here are some facts; you judge for yourself. California did have a mild climate. Mexicans already owned large ranches, but there was plenty of land left. The soil was rich, the people few. There were vast stretches of land where nobody lived. The men who first reached California's inland valleys could stake out ranches as big as the smallest state in the East. And the lush meadows of Oregon's Willamette Valley beckoned the farmer too.

In 1837, times were hard in the Mississippi Valley. The Happy Land of the Pacific Coast tempted many a farmer to start loading his wagon for the trip. How did he get there? That's another story!

THE START OF THE OREGON TRAIL

If you were to travel from the middle of the United States to the West Coast today, you'd hop on a jet plane. It would take less than 3 hours to go from the Missouri River to Portland, Oregon. How long do you think it took to travel the same distance on the Oregon Trail?

"Three months?"

More like 4 to 6 months. But you can still see the old trail, if your plane dips low enough. You can see the ruts made by the thousands of covered wagons that passed over it 130 years ago. The trail was first traveled in 1812. This was over 30 years before the famous old wagon trains carried families on their way to find new homes in the West. The trail was blazed by the Astorians, fur traders working for John Jacob Astor. On their way east they found South Pass, the lowest, easiest way through the Rockies. That's where the trail, and later the railroads, crossed the Great Divide.

The first Americans to go west on the trail were Nathaniel Wyeth and his men in 1832. Wyeth was a Boston businessman who dreamed of making a fortune with a trading post in Oregon. He took a wagon that became a boat when it was turned

The West was won with the help of wagons. They were called prairie schooners, or Conestoga wagons after the city where they were built. The pioneers usually traveled in wagon trains (below) for better protection against Indian attacks.

80

upside down. But it had to be left at St. Louis. Wyeth's dream of building a big business at the mouth of the Columbia River was no more realistic than his wagon-boat. But though he failed, he sparked other people's interest in the Oregon Trail.

THE FIRST MISSIONARIES

The Far West was rugged country and it took rugged men to tame it—trappers, traders, fighters, adventurers. But in the 1830's a new breed took to the trail.

"Farmers? Cowboys?"

No, but they were soon to follow. The new pioneers were missionaries. They were not trying to make their fortunes. A different purpose drove them to endure the hardships of the trail. They wanted to convert the Indians to Christianity.

Jason and Daniel Lee were the first missionaries to Oregon. Like other ministers, Jason had been stirred by a tale that four Indians had come to St. Louis begging for a white preacher to teach them the Bible. Nathaniel Wyeth took the Lees' group with him on his second overland trip in 1834. On the way, they stopped and built Fort Hall on the Snake River— an important station on the trail.

At Fort Vancouver, near modern Portland, they were welcomed by Dr. McLoughlin of Hudson's Bay Company. About 20 British, French, and Indian families, former trappers for the English company, were farming in the nearby Willamette Valley. Jason Lee took one look at the lush meadows of the Willamette. "We'll put the mission right here," he said, and began building his log cabin.

"Did Oregon belong to England or to the United States?"

Well, nobody knew. The English already had their trading post, Fort Vancouver, where the Columbia and Willamette rivers joined. They considered Oregon as England's. But the American fur traders and missionaries wanted Oregon to be American. So the Lees and other missionaries waged a campaign to bring settlers to Oregon. Of course, they were

converting Indians. But they believed that saving souls and saving Oregon for the United States deserved equal time.

A BRIDE GOES WEST

Some call Marcus Whitman, missionary-doctor, "the man who saved Oregon." But. . . .

"Were there any girl missionaries?"

I'm coming to that. Whitman started for Oregon with Sam Parker in 1835. Beyond South Pass, where Whitman removed the arrow from Jim Bridger, Sam went on. But Whitman turned back for something he needed.

"Extra preachers? Wagons?"

Yes, and something he needed more—a wife. He married lovely redheaded Narcissa. In 1836 they started out with another couple, the Spaldings. Mr. Spalding had wanted to marry Narcissa but she turned him down. He married Eliza—thin, sickly, and deeply religious. On their honeymoon, Marcus and Narcissa were very happy. Spalding looked at them grimly and prayed for Narcissa's soul. He said it wasn't Christian to be so lively and gay.

Like other missionaries, they had mountain men, Tom Fitzpatrick and Black Harris, for guides. The guides drove hard along the Platte, hurrying to the rendezvous. Narcissa mostly rode sidesaddle, which was the custom of ladies at that time. Sometimes she drove the light wagon while sickly Eliza rested in back. The wagon jolted horribly across the gullies. At Fort Laramie the women finally got a chance to do their washing. Then they pressed on to South Pass.

Evenings, Narcissa baked bread in the campfire's embers. Afternoons, she gave tea parties, with tea served from tin basins. Her tablecloth was a rubber sheet spread out on the prairie. Perched on her husband's knee, she sliced her bread with the trapper's knife that hung from her belt and passed it to the grizzled mountain men. They were charmed by her.

The pioneer families who traveled westward experienced great hardships. Often they risked death from Indian ambushes along trails or in mountain gorges, and women as well as men had to know how to shoot a gun. For the entire length of the journey, the covered wagon was home. By day the family traveled. At night men took turns standing guard while the others slept.

The heart of a mining town was the saloon (above). Here men drank, fought, and gambled, often losing all the gold they had so painstakingly mined. When nearby rivers yielded no more gold, once-bustling cities became ghost towns like Eureka, Colorado (opposite).

After South Pass came the rendezvous. Tom stopped there, and British guides took over for the last and roughest part. At Fort Hall they told Marcus to leave the wagon. No wagon had ever gone past here. Marcus said the wagon must go through for Narcissa's sake—she was pregnant now. So down gulches and up Snake River cliffs the wagon went. An axle broke. Marcus made a cart for Narcissa from the other axle. But at Fort Boise he had to give up. The first white women to travel the trail rode sidesaddle over the Blue Mountains. Then they took a boat to Fort Vancouver.

"Was the baby all right?"

Fine. The next spring at Marcus' mission near Walla Walla the Whitmans' daughter, Alice, was born. She was the first white American baby born in Oregon.

A PERILOUS JOURNEY

"What about pioneers to California?"

John Marsh, California enthusiast, wrote letters telling everyone to come to his earthly paradise. It was always spring. There was no malaria. Of course, to get there you had to travel thousands of miles of trail. Part of it ran through desert crawling with scorpions, tarantulas, rattlesnakes—and maybe even hostile Indians.

Nevertheless, 500 people signed up in 1840 to go to California. Alarmed merchants spread horror stories about the trip. Their campaign succeeded so well that by departure time in May, less than 70 people

appeared for the trip. They had horses, a few wagons, and wheelbarrows loaded with goods. Their maps were outdated, and they knew nothing about what they faced.

Their leader was 22-year-old John Bidwell. John Bartleson was elected commander, but he was not a strong leader. Luckily the party fell in with mountain man Tom Fitzpatrick. But Tom was heading for Oregon. When he turned north at Soda Springs, half the party stayed with him and the Oregon Trail. The rest,

32 people, struck out into the desert with no guide and only the vaguest advice. They should find Great Salt Lake, pass north of it, and go west, they had been told. If they veered south, they'd be lost in the desert; if too far north, they'd be trapped in ravines.

Wagons, stuck in Utah sands, had to be left behind. The pioneers loaded their possessions on horses and mules. Women and children trudged on foot under the blazing sun. Horses strayed or starved. The remaining ones grew skeleton-thin.

Somehow the little band found the Humboldt River and followed it west. October 16, 5 months after they started, they came up against the towering wall of the Sierra Nevada. Snow glistened on the peaks. Was it too late to cross? Would they have to go back to Fort Hall?

CALIFORNIA AT LAST

The Bidwell party voted to go on and brave the mountains. They met an Indian who offered to guide them. He led them over paths so dangerously narrow that a few overloaded horses fell over the cliff. Sometimes they had to hoist mules up the canyons with ropes. Food was so scarce that to keep from starving they killed and ate one mule. Finally they saw a river running west and followed it down to the San Joaquin Valley. Here they found food—luscious grapes to pick and antelope to hunt.

On November 4 they came to a cluster of ramshackle cabins. This was their goal —the John Marsh Ranch at Mount Diablo (near present-day San Francisco). Marsh was glad to see them and fed them well.

But was this the paradise Marsh had written home about? These bare huts—no orchards, no gardens? What disappointment!

Still, they knew they were lucky to be alive. And all of them were proud to belong to the first party to complete the overland route to California.

THE GREAT MIGRATION BEGINS

In 1842, the year after the Bidwell party had set out for California, the Rev. Elijah White was appointed Oregon Indian agent. With Tom Fitzpatrick's help, he took the first large group of people (over 100) to Oregon. Many took dogs. Those without dogs feared the barking would attract Indians, and soon threats of "You shoot my dog and I'll shoot you" echoed over the prairies. But dogs and men got through.

White brought Dr. Whitman a letter telling him to abandon one of his missions. Whitman rode furiously back east. All winter he lectured audiences and tried to influence officials, always with one mes-

The history of the West is filled with tales of adventurers and bandits. But there were also many men, such as Marshal "Wild Bill" Hickok of Abilene and Wyatt Earp, who sought to uphold the law.

sage: "If you want Oregon to be American, you'd better fill it with Americans."

Oregon fever was rising. Glowing reports spread, the Happy Land beckoned— and the people came. They gathered 1,000 strong at Independence, Missouri, in May, 1843. The covered wagons were about to roll—a whole village of them at once!

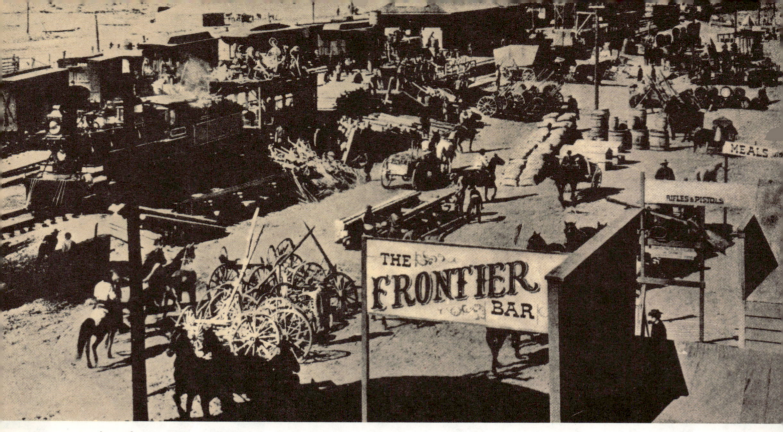

A settlement of workers who built the trunk line for the Union Pacific Railroad about 1865.

PIONEERS MAKE RULES

Independence (near what is now Kansas City) was the takeoff point. People milled about, buying food, cattle, prairie schooners, all in a rush to get started.

"Sounds like a mob."

Not for long. At Elm Wood they reached the frontier. Law stopped here—and the people stopped, too, to make their own law. All men 16 and over could vote (sorry, no women) and they voted by lining up behind their choice. The man with the longest line of voters won. They elected a leader, Peter Burnett; an orderly sergeant, J. W. Nesmith; and a council to settle fights and act as a jury. This was the first party to organize itself like an army or a town. They split into two columns— a fast "light column" and a slow "cow column," for 5,000 cows and oxen were going, too. Late in May, the Great Migration began to roll across the plains.

A DAY WITH THE WAGON TRAIN

Two days out, the trail forked. One sign said "Santa Fe." The "light column" —60 wagons and few animals—turned toward the sign that said "Road to Oregon." Slowly the wagons of the "cow column," surrounded by herds and clouds of dust, rumbled after.

The "cows'" captain, Jesse Applegate, described trail life in his now-famous book, *A Day With the Cow Column*. At daybreak watchmen woke everyone. People came out of tents and wagons and started breakfast fires. They milked cows and let them out to graze on the prairie. At 7 o'clock the bugle blew. Drivers yelled at oxen and yanked squeaky wagons into line, forming a column a mile long. The column was split into four companies that changed positions each day, so that each took turns getting the suffocating dust of last place.

Leaders walked with their line of oxen. Women and children picked flowers along the edge of the trail. Extra horsemen rode behind as guards. Far ahead galloped the pilot, marking difficult spots. Sometimes the women made the line stop at a spring for laundry and baths. Noon lunch was light, and the march kept on till sunset.

Below: A group of prospectors headed for California in search of gold in 1880. Although the days of the famous gold rush were past, many still hoped to find their fortunes in western rivers.

Then they halted while the pilot traced a circle 100 yards wide. Drivers parked their wagons along the circle, chaining them together to make a barricade. Oxen couldn't break out, and Indians or wolves couldn't break in.

Inside their fort, the women fixed a hot dinner of salted meat, pancakes, coffee. As darkness fell, everyone chattered and sang around the campfire. Soon voices stilled and the camp slept.

Sometimes hurricanes toppled wagons. Sometimes herds of buffalo charged the line and had to be stopped with bonfires. But babies were born, lovers met, old people died, and the wave of pioneers rolled on to Oregon.

WAGONS GET THROUGH!

The pioneers soon saw they were carrying far too many possessions. The Oregon Trail was littered with discarded bedsteads, iron stoves, boxes of books. Women found long trailing dresses a nuisance on the trail. They tucked their skirts up as far as they dared. They threw away finery or traded it to the Snake squaws.

But, like turtles, they were carrying their homes with them, and they had to have wagons. So at Fort Hall, when the guides said what they always said, "No wagons past here," there were shouts of dismay.

"Marcus Whitman would have said...."

Marcus was there, and he said it: "The wagons must go through!"

"He was wrong before."

This time was different. Never before had such an army come along the trail. Men and boys surged out in front of the wagon train. They filled up holes, leveled rough places, hauled trees out of the way. They found spots along the stream where wagons could cross. Foot by foot they built the road through the wilds of the Snake River, across the Blue Mountains. They built it right in front of their oncoming wagon wheels! And wagons got through to Oregon at last.

They reached Whitman's Walla Walla mission in October. By spring they were already farming on the Willamette. After them came many caravans—3,000 people

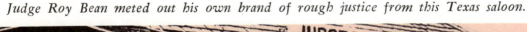

Judge Roy Bean meted out his own brand of rough justice from this Texas saloon.

Pioneers resting in the forest along a trail leading west.

in 1845, doubling the population. How could Oregon be English now? As Marcus had hoped, enough Americans marched into Oregon to make it a United States territory. It became so in 1848.

SHORTCUT TO CALIFORNIA?

Jealous California boosters watched the crowds going to Oregon, while only a few men came their way. One, Lansford Hastings, hoped to become important in politics, first in California and then nationally. For that he needed settlers. Maybe a shortcut would lure pioneers. He studied the map. Instead of looping far north to Fort Hall, wagons should cut south of Salt Lake from Fort Bridger and head right across Utah. Why, you could make it in 120 days—much more quickly than to Oregon!

This was the Hastings Cutoff. It seemed short on the map, but it went through the desert. The first people who tried it ex-

91

A Pony Express rider greets some friends.

pected to cross the desert in 24 hours. They trudged on day after day. Animals fell to the ground or went mad with thirst. When at last the travelers struggled out, they had to take grass and water 30 miles back to the surviving horses. Old-timers say that Utah's bluish haze is what's left of the curses those suffering men called down on Hastings and his shortcut.

THE SAINTS GO TO UTAH

How would you like to go to Deseret? "That sounds like more desert."

It looked like desert, too. But Deseret was the word the Mormons used for "honeybee," and the Saints made Deseret blossom like a bee's heaven. The Saints got their name because they belonged to the Church of Jesus Christ of Latter-Day Saints, started by Joseph Smith in 1830. We know them as Mormons. Conflicts with neighbors led to Smith's murder, and the Saints knew they would have to go west to find a place of their own.

Under the leadership of Brigham Young, the Pioneer Band, with 146 young people, took to the trail in 1847. When they reached Fort Bridger, Jim Bridger laughed at their plans. Nothing could live in the desert but tarantulas! This suited the party. If nobody wanted that land, perhaps they would be left in peace there.

They pressed on through the Wasatch Mountains and Emigration Canyon. Below they saw the Great Salt Lake. Young pointed and said: "This is the place."

Nothing looked less like the Promised Land than this barren sagebrush valley. But they dammed a stream, flooded land, and planted crops. Soon 1,500 more Saints came. By fall there were 4,000. The next year their numbers more than doubled.

In 1848 they were farming 5,000 acres. And then the crickets came—millions of them. The fields were black with them, eating the grain crop. Would a mere insect destroy the Saints after all their heartbreaking work? The Saints prayed for help.

Suddenly in flew a seagull—and an-

92

other and another. The Saints stared in amazement. Gulls, so far from the sea? The gulls settled over the hot fields in waves of flapping wings, feasting on crickets. The crop was saved!

Today in Salt Lake City you can see the Seagull Monument that the grateful Saints put up to honor their rescuers.

They called their colony Deseret. We call it the state of Utah.

Above: Brigham Young, head of the Mormons, who led his followers in search of a safe land. They settled in the area around Great Salt Lake. Below: Map showing the route of the Pony Express. The messengers covered the distance between St. Joseph, Missouri, and Sacramento, California, in about 9 days, riding 75 miles a day and changing horses every 15 miles.

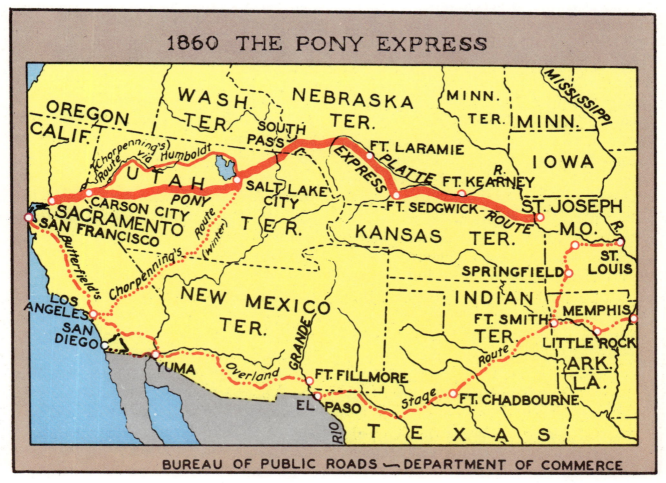

1860 THE PONY EXPRESS

BUREAU OF PUBLIC ROADS — DEPARTMENT OF COMMERCE

TRAPPED IN THE SNOW

In the early 1840's a trickle of pioneers reached California. Some came through Oregon and then headed south to the Sacramento Valley. Others followed the trail blazed by Joseph Walker, entering the San Joaquin Valley by Walker Pass. In 1844 the Stevens-Murphy party had the honor of being the first to get wagons through to California.

The year 1846 marks the blackest tragedy in the story of California migration. That spring George and Jacob Donner led a well-organized caravan out of Independence. Most of the people were related, in several large families. One report says there were 26 men, 12 women, and 33 children—a very high proportion of young people. Others number the party at 87 or 89 altogether.

All went well as far as Fort Bridger. There they found a note from Lansford Hastings urging them to use his shortcut and save time. The caravan with them went on north to Fort Hall. But the Donners, the Reeds, and the Breen family chose the Hastings Cutoff. Why go the long way round if you could get there in a hurry?

But it took 30 days instead of the 12 they had counted on to reach the valley south of Great Salt Lake. They lost their way. They camped too long—once waiting 8 days for Hastings, who never came. They took 64 hours to cross the blazing desert. Also, they had to retrace their steps at one point to save their animals and bring them along.

In the arid Humboldt region, sand blowing in their eyes and a water shortage made everyone tense and irritable. Violence broke out. One man killed another. They were beginning to worry about being late for the mountain crossing. But none of them realized that the clock was ticking their lives away.

They had already lost a month's time before they reached the Sierras. Snow-capped peaks loomed before them. It was late fall, they knew. What they didn't know was that winter was coming unusually early this year. But they saw the snow begin to sift down as they started along the precipitous trails toward the high pass we now call Donner Pass.

It was Halloween before they made camp in a trapper's shanty beside a body of water they called Truckee's Lake. Long and narrow, walled in by cliffs, today it is named Donner Lake in their memory.

That night the snow struck with full fury. Winds howled and drifts piled up. By morning, most of the cattle had wandered away. Many were buried under snow and the Donners were unable to find them in spite of their desperate need for meat.

Some of the men went out to hunt for the mountain pass. They came back with bitter news. The pass was blocked by snowdrifts 7 feet deep!

They finally faced the terrible truth: they were snowbound in the Sierras. They built huts of wagon covers and underbrush and huddled together in the bone-breaking cold. What cattle they could find, they killed for food. That was all they had and it would soon be gone.

By mid-December they knew something had to be done or they would perish. In desperation, 15 men and women on homemade snowshoes started out on a mission to seek help. Those left behind ran out of beef. They gnawed tree bark and chewed boiled cowhide. Death from starvation hung over them.

Not until February 19 did the first re-

Snow-capped mountain peaks and high mountain passes added to the dangers that faced the early pioneers in their westward search for a new homeland and a new life.

lief party get through with food. In March, when rescuers brought them out, only 45 of the group were still alive.

THE BEAR FLAG REVOLT

California, like Utah, belonged to Mexico. The difference is that Utah was uninhabited when the Saints came. But the Mexicans had a thriving colony along California's coast, and they wanted to keep it. Now land-hungry Americans were moving into the Sacramento and Sonoma valleys, starting great ranches. The restless Americans chafed under Mexican control. Trouble lay ahead.

It began early in 1846. John C. Frémont was in California on his third exploring trip, guided by mountain man Kit Carson. General Castro, the Mexican military commander, ordered Frémont to leave the coast. A fight threatened but no

Above: On May 10, 1869, two lines of the railroad uniting East and West met at Promontory, Utah. In a commemorative ceremony, the governor of California joined the lines with a gold spike. The spike was inscribed: "May God protect the unity of our country as this railroad united two great Oceans."

blood was shed. Soon rebellious settlers in the Sacramento Valley asked Frémont for help. He agreed. The rebels seized some horses and kidnapped a wealthy Mexican rancher.

Excitement grew when they heard Castro was sending troops to wipe out the settlers. Frémont called the rebels together at Sonoma. They declared independence from Mexico, seized the fort, and raised their own flag over it. The flag had a bear on it and the words "California Republic."

But the "Bear Flag Republic" didn't last long. Almost at once their revolt was swallowed up in the Mexican War. When it ended in 1848, California and the Southwest were American territory.

GOLD IN CALIFORNIA

In the Sacramento Valley, John Sutter reigned over a ranch as big as a small kingdom. For miles around his herds grazed, his orchards and vineyards throve. In January, 1848, his men were building a sawmill and flour mill on the American River. Mills would make Sutter's Fort still richer.

Digging into the river to enlarge the mill, James Marshall saw something gleam in the water. He picked it up—a rock with a dull yellow shine. His heart beat faster. Could it be what he thought it was?

He raced to Sutter's office. Making sure no one else heard them, he showed Sutter his yellow rock. Sutter weighed it and tested it with acid. No doubt about it— Marshall had found gold!

Sutter went to see for himself. All his men were picking up these nuggets. He saw a golden streak in a boulder. He could pry gold out with his knife, almost enough gold to make a ring.

But Sutter was not happy. If this news became known, who would stay and build

his mill? His men promised to keep the secret.

But a secret like that couldn't be kept for long. Millworkers' children played with the pretty yellow rocks. Men who weren't in on the secret saw them playing, looked at the rocks—and took them to Sam Brannan.

Sam, a Mormon, ran a general store near the fort. When a man offered to pay for his flour and bacon with a nugget, Sam's eyes got very big. If men came here hunting gold, imagine how much trade his store would have!

That May, Sam ran along the streets of San Francisco waving a fistful of nuggets. "Gold," he shouted, "gold from the American River!"

The news raged through the city like a fire. People put down their tools, left their shops, and rode off to the Sacramento Valley. Sailors deserted their ships until the bay was clogged with masts. A kind of madness struck the region, and soon men were overrunning Sutter's land like an army of elephants. Sutter's fields were crushed beneath their boots.

Sutter was ruined. No more work in orchards and mills. The California gold rush had begun!

THE FORTY-NINERS

The next year, the forty-niners hit California like a tidal wave. President Polk had announced the discovery of gold in his December, 1848, message to Congress. Within a month, 61 ships carrying gold hunters were on their way around South America. Gold fever swept the land, spreading like smallpox.

By the end of May, 12,000 wagons had crossed the Missouri. An army of over 40,000 forty-niners plodded along the 97 overland trails. Marchers were strung out for miles and miles. All had dreams of "striking it rich" and becoming millionaires overnight. Around their campfires they sang a new popular song:

Oh, Susanna,
    Don't you cry for me.
I'm off to California
    With my washbowl on my knee.

(A washbowl was a bowl for panning gold.)

Most knew nothing of pioneering. Many died—5,000 in a cholera outbreak. Others were lost in the desert or were caught in Sierra snows. But the rest came on like an avalanche—some across the jungles of the Isthmus of Panama, and others by ship around Cape Horn (the southernmost tip of South America).

Overnight the little village of Yerba Buena (now San Francisco) turned into a big brawling city of gambling dens and saloons. From this point, the forty-niners fanned out into the canyons of the Sierra foothills east of Sacramento. True, gold swirled in the streams and veined the rocks. Each man staked his claim on a length of river and began panning gold with his "washbowl" or any other pan. He stood in the icy stream, swirled sand and water in the pan, let the water run off, and picked nuggets or gold dust from the sand. His home was a cabin or tent in towns that sprang up like mushrooms— Hangtown, Skunk Gulch, Red Dog, Poker Flat, Hell's Delight.

But easy come, easy go. He could make a fortune in a day and lose it that night at the gambling table. And the cost of living went up—eggs cost $10 a dozen! The people who really became rich were the merchants and gamblers. The miners didn't care, however. They were crazy for gold. After all, it was *free*; just pick it up!

The gold rush drew men from all over the world. Americans, British, Mexicans, Frenchmen, Australians, South Americans, Chinese, and Germans all mingled in the mining camps. At first men were so honest that nothing was ever locked up. But then outlaws came. Miners took care of them very quickly. The nearest men formed a jury and decided the case. If the verdict was "guilty," they either chased the outlaw out of camp or strung him up to the nearest tree.

Now California had 100,000 people— more than any place west of Texas!

Bloody battles between the Mexicans and Texans were fought near this fort in Texas.

THE LAST FRONTIER

"Say, Donald, you've told about trappers and miners and Indians—and not a word about cowboys. What's a Western story without cowboys?"

Well, Daisy, the day of the cowboy reached its high point a bit later, in the 1870's and 1880's. The "cattle kingdom" really began when Texas rebelled against Mexico in 1836. Until Texas joined the Union in 1845, it was a republic, and its flag had one star, which accounts for its present nickname, the Lone Star State. This was a period of border wars between Texans and Mexicans around the Rio Grande. When a Mexican ranchero was forced to "vamoose" (leave suddenly), the Texans would take everything he'd left. That included his herds of cattle.

This was the start of the "cattle kingdom." The herds increased rapidly and spread into the region that became Oklahoma, Kansas, Nebraska, the Dakotas, Wyoming, Montana, Nevada, Utah, and New Mexico. The range was open then, no fenced-in pastures. And wherever the herds ranged, cowboys galloped beside them.

COWBOYS

Let's take a good look at the word "cowboy." It's not quite accurate because, first, the fellow who herded cattle was a man, not a boy. Second, the animals in his herd were not all cows, although that's what he called them. "Cow" means a female that has borne a calf. But cowboys herded bulls, steers, and mavericks, too.

"What's a maverick?"

That's a calf at least 2 years old that hasn't been branded yet—which meant that whoever found it could claim it.

Herds wandered all over the range, wherever they could find good grass. The cowboy's job was to keep them together for the rancher. Otherwise the herds could become widely separated on the vast prairie.

Mexican cowboys (*vaqueros*) knew this. They taught Americans how to herd cattle on horseback. From them our cowboys learned how to use the tools of their trade—the lasso, the high-pommeled western saddle, the spurs, and the branding

On the preceding pages are some familiar scenes in the West: Cowboys heading home after a long day in the saddle, and (opposite page) a cattle roundup.

Seals representing three periods in the colorful history of the state of Texas. Left to right: Texas seals during Spanish, French, and Mexican rule. Opposite page: The museum at Aquarena Spring, Texas, housed in an old mansion, contains fascinating displays of important events in the state's history.

irons. In the beginning, cowboys were called "cow hunters."

And what "cows"! They were descendants of the Andalusian cattle brought to Mexico by the Spanish conquistadores (conquerors). As the years passed, the cattle multiplied and ran in wild herds north of the Rio Grande, in what became Texas. Because of their long sharp horns, twisted upward like handlebars, they were called longhorns.

The longhorn was a very tough beast. He was so ferocious that people said he was "more fearful than five buffaloes put together." He was supposed to be able to run hundreds of miles tirelessly, without water. Exaggeration? Maybe. But I wouldn't want to face an angry longhorn, would you?

"With cattle running all over the place, how did a man know which were his?"

That, my friends, is where branding comes in. The spring and autumn round-ups were the big days in a cowboy's life. In the spring the longhorns were herded back to the ranch. Then cowboys "cut" calves out of the herd. (That meant riding into the mass of animals and pushing a calf out into the open where the cowboys could get to him.) All calves under 2 years old had to be branded with the ranch's special mark, or brand.

The cowboy roped his calf and wrestled it down to the ground. Then he pressed the white-hot branding iron (in the shape of the ranch's mark) against

the calf's flank for half a minute. This singed the hide and left a permanent scar —a "label" telling everybody whose animal it was. According to the cowboys, this didn't really hurt the calf much. But it would be interesting to hear what the calf had to say about that.

BRONCO BUSTING

If you think longhorns were wild, you should have seen the horses that were used to herd them.

The way to get hold of a horse was to ride out on the range and find a mustang, or bronco (Spanish for "wild"). These

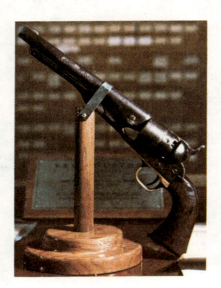

The museum at Huntsville, Texas, is filled with fascinating memorabilia of the life of Sam Houston, hero of Texan independence. Of special interest are the portrait of Houston, his gold pen and diary, and his pistol.

mustangs were descendants of the horses Spaniards brought to the New World. Many horses escaped from their masters and joined the vast herds of mustangs that ran wild on the prairies.

The cowboy roped his bronco colt and forced it back to the ranch, where he fenced it inside the corral. (A corral is a circle that may be as wide as 50 feet in diameter. It is enclosed by high wooden stakes driven into the ground, with crossbars between the stakes for extra protec-

tion.) The cowboy blindfolded the colt. Then he put a saddle on its back and strapped it on firmly. Remember, this bronco had never before felt anything heavier than a butterfly on its back! But if the colt felt the saddle was an insult, you should see how it reacted to what happened next. This man had the nerve to jump into the saddle and try to *sit* on the bronco!

That was the signal for a battle of wills. The cowboy was determined to ride. The colt was determined never to be ridden. It whinnied, bucked, reared, kicked, and bolted around the corral. It turned itself into a pretzel made of lightning, changing shape every second. The cowboy wrapped his legs around the colt and hung on for dear life as long as he could. Sometimes that wasn't very long. When he got thrown off, he had to roll out of the way of the flying hooves in a hurry. The colt would have loved to trample him.

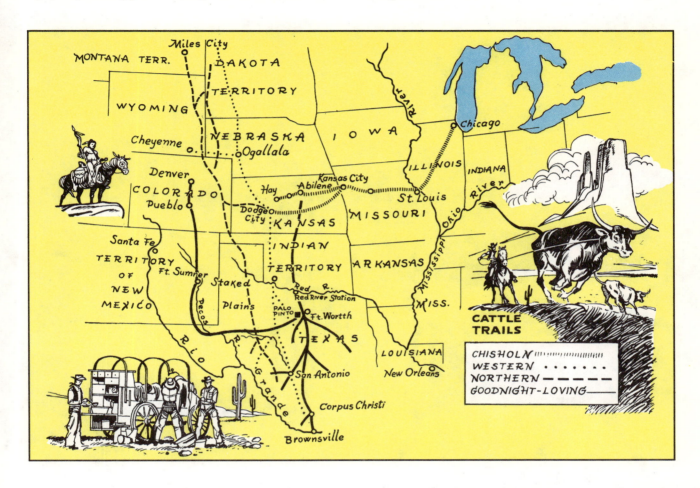

On the following page: With the enormous growth of the cattle industry after the Civil War, ways had to be found to transport vast herds from ranches and grazing grounds to shipping points and markets. Gradually special routes, or trails, were developed, and every year cowboys drove their herds along the trails. One of the most famous of these routes was the Chisholm Trail, probably named for Jesse Chisholm, a half-breed Cherokee Indian who, in 1866, drove his wagon, loaded with buffalo hides, through Oklahoma to Kansas. Other trails were the Western, Northern, and Goodnight–Loving. For almost 2 decades they were the means by which cattle reached the distant slaughterhouses. The trails are part of the rich folklore of the West, long celebrated in both song and story. The trip along the trail required a great deal of courage and endurance. Often the cowboys had to lead tens of thousands of head of cattle through territory filled with hostile Indians and dangerous outlaws. There were rapid rivers to ford, and severe sand- and windstorms to be endured. The greatest task of all was to keep the gigantic herd calm at all times, for the slightest scare was sometimes enough to drive the animals frantic with fear and cause them to stampede wildly across the plains. The nights were lonely and frightening. Occasionally the cries of fierce animals pierced the stillness, and the herds stirred restlessly. It was during these dark hours that the weary cowboys gathered around their campfires and sang, to the accompaniment of their guitars, the melancholy ballads that became their trademark.

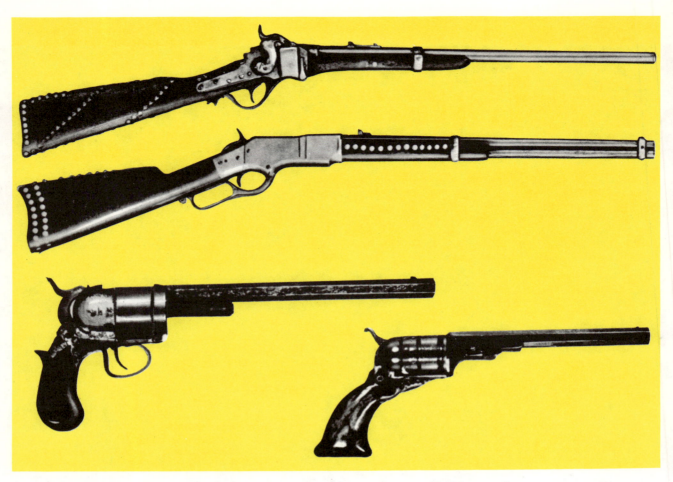

In their early encounters with the Indians, the white men, armed with superior weapons, were confident that they could easily overcome their opponents, whose only combat experience had been with simple bows and arrows. But within a short time the white men were to learn that their hopes for an early victory were ill-founded. For although it was true that their weapons were much more sophisticated than those of their enemies, they were far less suited to the kind of combat in which they were used.

When the two groups met in battle, the white men found that they were faced with many unforeseen difficulties. Their firearm was the long rifle, which had to be loaded after each shot. In order to reload, the fighters had to dismount. Although the entire maneuver took only a few minutes, this was sufficient time for the Indians to attack with a rapid volley of dozens of arrows, and to gallop hundreds of yards across the prairie well beyond the reach of a rifle's range.

It was not until the invention of the repeater weapon that the situation changed. This innovation removed the necessity for dismounting and reloading after each firing, and made it much easier for the white men to conquer the Indians.

Perhaps the most famous weapon designed for combat on horseback was the Colt six-shooter, named for its inventor, Samuel Colt. When Colt was 16 years old, he signed on as a sailor on the Boston-Calcutta route, and during the long crossing he passed the time whittling gun models. One of the guns he devised was a revolver, a weapon with a several-chambered cylinder that would eliminate the necessity for reloading after each firing.

In 1836 Colt patented his revolver and opened a factory to manufacture it. At first the government was cool to the new weapon, but orders began to pour in from the Republic of Texas for guns to use in the war against the Mexicans. The Texas orders were not enough to keep the factory in business, however, and Colt was forced into bankruptcy. When the government finally decided to order the gun, Colt had run out of money, and was forced to close his factory. Determined not to miss out on the government order, he designed an improved model and set up a new factory in Connecticut. In a few short years, Samuel Colt had amassed a fortune.

The guns pictured are (top to bottom): Sharps Rifle (1874); Winchester Rifle (1866); Modified Colt Army Revolver (1872); Colt New Navy Double-Action Revolver (1899).

110

Sometimes man and colt fought for several weeks before the mustang decided to accept its new job. This process was called breaking a colt to saddle, or bronco busting. Not all colts could be broken. Those who refused were called outlaws. They were used in rodeos where cowboys put on shows of horsemanship.

Once broken, a horse was trained for special jobs. The best animals were used as "cow horses." A cow horse could take off at a gallop in a instant, stop on a dime, and gallop like the wind all day without water. Such a horse was the cowboy's best friend. He had forgotten the battle in the corral, and he obeyed his rider's signals as if he were a mind-reader.

Sometimes a horse got very sick or suffered an incurable wound. In that case, he would have to be put out of his misery with a bullet between the eyes. Often a cowboy couldn't bring himself to do this. He would call for help by firing his six-shooter into the air. Then another cowboy, hearing the signal, would come and carry out the sad task.

A POET AT HEART

"Did the cowboy just go off and leave his poor horse where it fell?"

No. He carefully dug a grave and buried his horse on the prairie. He marked the grave with a slate tombstone. On it he crudely scratched out an epitaph:

HERE LIES
"I'M HERE"
The best of horses
A hardy little gentleman
Died in this place
September 3, 1890

or:

HERE LIES
"WHAT NEXT"
Died July 16, 1892

HE HAD THE BODY OF A HORSE
THE SOUL OF A KNIGHT OF OLD
AND THE LOVE OF MAN
WHO ERECTED THIS TOMBSTONE

or:

JIM
A REAL HORSE
1 October 1892

You can see that our rough, tough cowboy was a poet at heart. Why not? He lived close to nature. That meant living with beauty, and always the threat of danger.

THE COWBOY'S BEST FRIEND

The cowboy spent most of his life on horseback. He never left his horse until it was time to eat or sleep. You would almost have thought he and his horse were one, like the centaur. (The centaur was a creature half-man, half-horse, that existed in old Greek myths.) The cowboy's legs might seem a bit curved from straddling the horse, which gave him a strange rolling walk. But he never walked if he could help it. The farthest he would go on foot was from the bunkhouse where he slept to the corral and back again.

His horse was like a human friend or a brother. He shared all he had with his horse just as he would with another cowboy. Sometimes on the hot dusty plains the cowboy would drink the juice from a can of tomatoes, then feed the tomatoes to his horse.

The cowboy's saddle was made just for him. Usually it fitted his body perfectly. He called it his "workbench." In a gambling game at the local saloon, he might lose all his money, his spurs, or even his gun, but never his saddle.

The saddle had a high horn, or pommel, in the front. The cowboy looped his lasso around this horn. If he needed to catch an escaping cow, he whirled the lasso around his head and sent it flying, catching the animal in the loop at the end.

After the autumn roundup the cowboy's job was to drive the herd to the nearest railroad depot. Since the depot might be hundreds of miles away, this process was called the Long Drive. He had to hold the herd together, keep it moving, and protect it from wolves, thieves, and other dangers. He sang to his cattle, for this kept them from getting frightened. Many of his songs became famous. Out of them developed some of the music that was later called "country-and-Western." He sang mostly about his work, about how

 . . . we round up the dogies,
We mark them and brand them and bob
    off their tails;
We load the chuck wagon and then throw
    the dogies upon the long trail—
Whoopee ti yi yo, git along little
    dogies. . . .

This song was called "Whoopee Ti Yi Yo," which was the refrain of most cowboy songs. "Dogies" were young motherless calves. The chuck wagon was the wagon with cooking utensils and food

The cowboys were responsible for arranging every aspect of the difficult task of transporting the huge herds of cattle along the dangerous trails. They worked hard, slept little, and had few moments of relaxation.

that followed the herds. When it was time to make camp, the cook made a fire and cooked "chuck," or dinner, for the cowboys.

Often he sang about his troubles in songs such as "The Old Chisholm Trail":

> I wake in the morning afore daylight,
> And afore I sleep the moon shines bright.
> Oh, it's bacon and beans most every day,
> I'd as soon be eating prairie hay.
> Feet in the stirrups, seat in the saddle,
> I rattle along with the longhorn cattle,
> No chaps, no slicker, pourin' down rain,
> I swear I'll never night-herd again.

Of course he never kept his threat. Wild horses couldn't have kept him from being back on the Long Drive next year.

This was the cowboy. A writer who knew him summed him up this way: "He lives on his horse like the Bedouins, fights on horseback like the knights of old, and is armed with a 'six-shooter': a strange new weapon that can be fired accurately with either hand. He swears like a Turk, drinks like a sponge, dresses like an actor and fights like a devil. He is gallant with women, reserved with strangers, generous with his friends and brutal with his enemies. He is a typical *Westerner*."

I don't know if there is a typical westerner. But the cowboy was certainly typical of our *idea* of the westerner.

Every cowboy had to be a courageous horseman. Rodeos were favorite places for exhibiting riding ability, and one of the most exciting contests was bronco busting. Only the best riders could sit an unbroken colt for more than a few minutes.

LOLA AND LOTTA

Now, Buffalo Bill began as a. . . .
"No! I want to hear about the women!"
All right, Daisy. Let's take Lola Montez. Already a famous dancer, she blazed like a comet during the gold rush in San Francisco in 1853. She wasn't a very good actress, but never mind. Forty-niners loved theater and adored wild, exciting ladies. Lola's big act was a "spider dance." She pretended tarantulas were crawling all over her. Try it and see how wildly you'd have to shake yourself to get the spiders off! Miners roared with delight and threw flowers and gold nuggets at her. (When they didn't like an act, they'd throw tomatoes and chairs.)

Soon other actresses and critics began making fun of her dance. One story says that Lola was furious and challenged a critic to a duel. Then she went off to Grass Valley to sulk. She is said to have kept a tame bear chained near her cabin. She gave parties for the miners and the mining camp wives hated her. But a little girl, Lotta Crabtree, loved to stay around her cabin and listen to her songs.

Lotta was 6 when Lola started teaching her to sing and dance. Soon a Grass Valley theater wanted a "fairy star" (child actress). Lotta, in an Irish costume, danced the jig Lola had taught her. Then, dressed in white like an angel, she sang a sad ballad. Miners cried and showered her with a hail of nuggets and coins.

By 1859 Lotta was the hit of the San Francisco stage. Lola vanished, but Lotta was the West's pet for 35 years.

SUNBONNET GIRLS

"But what about just plain women?"

There were no "just plain women" in the West. Women were scarce, so a wife was a great prize. The girl in the sunbonnet had to be strong and brave to survive. In the gold camp she lived in a tent, with packing crates for sides. On the Plains she lived in a sod house—one tiny room for the whole family.

There was plenty of meat but few vegetables. To keep her family from developing scurvy, caused by lack of vitamin C, she planted seeds she had brought from home—peas, beans, carrots. She picked wild fruits. Often she had no jars in which to preserve fruit, so she might cook it to a thin paste, dry it on a platter, and hang the flat cakes from the roof. She learned which wild plants were edible. In the Northwest she roasted camas roots, which Narcissa Whitman said tasted "like figs." One wife tasted Indian acorn bread, but rejected it when she found it contained crushed worms! Another learned to make coffee from dried dandelion roots.

She made her own candles and soap. She cooked the soap and did her wash in a big iron kettle over a fire in the yard. The water of the Southwest was very hard, bad for washing and with a terrible taste. To make it drinkable she had to boil it and flavor it.

The fireplace was the center of her life. It served for heat, light, and cooking. She tried never to let the fire go out, for matches were scarce and expensive. A spit for roasting meat hung over the fireplace. There were big black kettles for boiling stew and a skillet for flapjacks.

This rider is not a cowboy of the Old West, but a tourist guide for people traveling in the Grand Canyon. His clothes and gear are those of the prairie horsemen of the past.

117

She made bread from sourdough and baked it on a board propped up in front of the fire.

At night, exhausted, she and her family curled up in front of the fire on a mattress stuffed with corn husks or buffalo hair.

THE CURE WAS WORSE THAN THE DISEASE

"But what happened if someone got sick?"

That was the pioneer family's greatest fear. Doctors were scarce and so was medicine. Instead they searched for mint or they grew herbs in the backyard. If someone got shot, the doctor operated on a barroom table, with whiskey for the pa-tient to dull the pain. Many doctors were quacks who gave out wild remedies.

The Sunbonnet Girl had to be her family's doctor. People thought the worse a medicine tasted, the better it was for you. So her medicine chest had bitter alum, sulfur, and turpentine in it. Castor oil was a favorite. On the bright side, she made essence of peppermint from the mint her children gathered in the woods. For fever, she put a cold cloth on the victim's head, cabbage leaves on his feet, and gave him sage tea, rhubarb, and soda. If the fever stayed high, she'd put the patient into a tub of ice water. She had great faith in mustard plasters on the chest and onions on the feet. Juice of onion and tobacco squirted in the ear cured earaches. Gun-

A lone Indian rider stands outlined against the western sky at sunset.

powder in water helped sore eyes; mixed with lard, it was good for frostbite. That gives you the general idea.

"Do you mean to tell me they *lived* through those cures?"

Some didn't make it, Daisy, but the tough ones survived. One thing was certain—western children knew it never paid to get sick!

BUFFALO BILL AND THE FIRST "WESTERN"

Now can we talk about Buffalo Bill? I have a special reason.

"All right. But I still don't think you told us enough about women in the West."

But Daisy, that's because there weren't very many women in the West at first. Anyway I'm putting two books on the book list that are *only* about women, if you're interested. The story of the West is mainly a story of white men, Indians, and Spanish-Americans. That's the way it was and I can't do a thing about it.

Buffalo Bill's real name was William F. Cody. When he was 14 years old, he became a rider for the Pony Express.

"Was it the Pony Express that got the first mail through from the East to the West Coast?"

Horseback riding is still a very popular sport in the West. Many children learn to ride when they are quite young, and some are as comfortable on their mounts as eastern children are on bicycles. Horse shows, rodeos, and horse races attract large groups of spectators.

No, the first transcontinental mail reached the Pacific by the Butterfield Overland Stage in 1858. But the stage was very slow. To hurry things along, the Pony Express was organized in 1860. This was the way it worked:

There were hundreds of Pony Express stations at 15-mile intervals. They stretched from St. Joseph, Missouri, to Sacramento, California. Each rider galloped at top speed from one station to the next. Then he jumped onto a fresh horse and raced on. He rode about 75 miles until he reached the station where the next rider waited. He threw his mailbags to the new rider, who flung them onto his mustang and galloped away.

"Like a relay race?"

Exactly. In this way, teams of riders covered nearly 2,000 miles in 8 to 10 days. Bill Cody was one of about 100 riders. Some were teen-agers like himself. They earned high wages for the time—between $100 and $150 a month. In spite of Indians, robbers, and bad weather, they lost the mail only once in the 18 months that the Pony Express lasted. The most important news they carried was word of Lincoln's election in November, 1860. Of course they couldn't carry much mail —about 20 pounds at a time. It was a very expensive way to send mail: at first it cost $5 for a half ounce and later $1 for the same.

The Pony Express began April 3, 1860, and ended October 24, 1861, when the telegraph system was built. After that news could travel instantly, as it does today.

"So Bill was out of a job?"

He soon got another that suited his adventurous tastes. Not yet 20 years old, he became a scout for the Union Army in the Civil War. Later he was a scout during the Indian Wars and was nearly scalped several times. He guided tourists and scientists, helped develop cattle ranching in Nebraska, and experimented with irrigation on his ranch near Cody, Wyoming. He got the name "Buffalo Bill" when he supplied railroad workers with buffalo meat while they built the railroads west. The story is that he killed 4,000 buffalo in 17 months!

But he won his real fame as a master of show business. It occurred to him that he could cash in on the legend of the "Wild West." After all, he'd lived that story himself.

In 1883 he took his "Wild West Show" on tour through America and Europe. It had Indians, cowboys, bucking broncos, and buffalo. He rode in the show himself until shortly before he died in 1917.

His show was the first Western. He took the real life of the West—the cowboys, the gunfights, the "quick draw"—and made it popular entertainment. From this a big business grew. You see the result every time you watch a Western on TV.

This is the story of the West as it really happened. If you want to know where I got my information, here are some of the books I read:

Paul Angle, *The New Nation Grows* (Vol. 2).
D. Arnold, *Thunder in the Southwest*.
Ray Billington, *Westward Expansion*.
Dee Brown, *Gentle Tamers*.
B. A. Botkin, *Treasury of American Folklore*.
Dan Elbert Clark, *West in American History*.
Thomas Clark, *Frontier America*.
Bernard De Voto, *Across the Wide Missouri*.
Bernard De Voto, *Course of Empire*.
Howard R. Dreggs, *The Old West Speaks*.
M. H. Fishwick, *American Heroes, Myth and Reality*.
Charles Hamilton, *The Cry of the Thunderbird*.
John A. Hawgood, *America's Western Frontier*.
F. W. Hodge, *Handbook of American Indians North of Mexico*.
J. D. Horan and P. Sann, *Pictorial History of the Wild West*.
Robert W. Howard, *This is the West*.
J. W. McSpadden, *Pioneer Heroes*.
P. A. Rollins, *The Cowboy*.
Theodore Roosevelt, *Ranch Life and the Hunting Trail*.
Nancy Ross, *Westward the Women*.
F. J. Turner, *The Frontier in American History*.
Owen Wister, *The Virginian*.

Daisy and I both thank you for coming with us on this long trip west.

Love,
Donald

INDEX